Reawakening an American Dream

Reawakening
AN
AMERICAN DREAM

*Create Your Path
to Financial Freedom*

KEVIN J. PALMER

NEW YORK

LONDON • NASHVILLE • MELBOURNE • VANCOUVER

Reawakening an American Dream

Creating Your Path to Financial Freedom

Published in New York, New York, by Morgan James Publishing. Morgan James is a trademark of Morgan James, LLC. www.MorganJamesPublishing.com

Because of the dynamic nature of the Internet, any web addresses or links contained in this book may have changed since publication and may no longer be valid. The views expressed in this work are solely those of the author and do not necessarily reflect the views of the publisher, and the publisher hereby disclaims any responsibility for them.

In the event you use any of the information herein, the author assumes no responsibility for your actions, and hereby disclaims any liability to any party for loss, damage, disruption and such, from any cause.

The author of this book does not dispense medical advice or prescribe the use of any technique as a form of treatment for physical, emotional, or medical problems without the advice of a physician, either directly or indirectly. The intent of the author is only to offer information of a general nature to help in your quest for well- being. In the event you use any of the information in this book for yourself, which is your constitutional right, the author and the publisher assume no responsibility for your actions.

All characters, events and situations are fictional, even though research was done on real people. Any people depicted in stock imagery are being used for illustrative purposes only.

Print information available on the last page. Some of the material in this book was previously published in *The Quiet Rich*

ISBN 9781631951121 paperback
ISBN 9781631951138 eBook
Library of Congress Control Number: 2020934676

Cover Design by:
Christopher Kirk
www.GFSstudio.com

Interior Design by:
Chris Treccani
www.3dogcreative.net

Morgan James is a proud partner of Habitat for Humanity Peninsula and Greater Williamsburg. Partners in building since 2006.

Get involved today! Visit
MorganJamesPublishing.com/giving-back

To my dad, who once said:
"Every American deserves the right to build a dream."

CONTENTS

PUBLISHERS NOTE

Another book by Kevin J. Palmer, soon to be critically acclaimed, challenges economic injustice through self-empowerment. Here he demonstrates how your first million dollars can be made without compromising personal values or harming others, simply by using abilities already within you.

This Wealth Expert and Financial Freedom Activist, who opposes power in the hands of *too few*, divulges his cutting-edge research about people who quietly questioned authority, rejected hierarchies and undertook personal revolutions to acquire the enduring power of net worth.

This book not only provides inclusive ethnic and gender diversity but a profoundly greater *diversity of thought*. The results are enticing stories that illustrate how you can achieve economic prosperity and permanently improve your quality of life.

Financial liberty is tested daily as people unknowingly fall hostage to agendas that drain their potential. Here, it is reaffirmed that all of us can exercise inalienable rights to a better life by refusing intrusions from bureaucrats, corporations, or any self-serving assemblages that rob economic dignity.

Making millions is easy when you already have one, but the rich don't want you to know where to begin. In these pages, under the writing hand of Kevin J. Palmer, a former behavioral finance CEO whose work shaped Wall Street investment policies, your American Dream reach is finally expanded.

INTRODUCTION

Your road to abundance has begun. Within these pages, discover trailblazing principles that integrate personality and behavioral essentials into heightened emotional intelligence. It will change your life and deliver the dignity that comes with having financial freedom on personal terms.

Economic liberty has its basis in our country's history but all too often, ordinary people inadvertently become part of someone else's agenda and seemingly secure circumstances, like steady employment, arbitrarily end. Blind passivity can make others rich and put you at risk.

However, there are those who resist that status quo and gain power to determine their own destiny without changing who they are or compromising their values. What follows is an ultimate foray into economic literacy that brilliantly illuminates improved behavioral thinking, paving a way to wealth that is as unique as you.

These are not stories about billionaires with schemes so dubious, antitrust attorneys cannot decipher them or about techy IPO startups. Instead, you'll find a propelling landscape of motivationally evolving stories about everyday people who are the real economic engines of America, that I named—the Quiet Rich.

Beyond the headlines of celebrities making exceedingly rare fortunes, there are untold numbers of Americans who became millionaires by following intuitive drivers. That kind of wealth, which you'll learn about here, is rarely discussed because it wasn't achieved sensationally. Instead, it was earned fundamentally, with hard work, self-reliance, and decency.

What makes this book unique is you! Until now, wealth techniques have come from pedagogues declaring what they think will work for others. Here, you honor yourself and embrace who you truly are to create your own prosperity. Reading these stories will synthesize within you, the hidden secrets of first-time millionaires to naturally manifest your own exclusive financial genius!

Hundreds of Case Studies

The stories you're about to read feature composite characters based on the analysis of hundreds of case studies. As an industry leader with big Wall Street companies and CEO at a behavioral finance firm, I conducted years of research into cognitive influences that positioned people to attain wealth, in their own ways using intrinsic focus and fortitude.

Identifying this subset of unique millionaires during my early investigations, I began calling them *the Quiet Rich* to honor them. These common people were called by an inner power—like the one within you—to turn steady intuitiveness into operant financial wisdom.

Like them, you can make your first million dollars by accentuating personality traits using their Secret Success Standards as stepping-stones.

Any Personality Type Can Succeed

From the outset of Carl Jung's early theories, much work in behavioral science has been done to classify people into psychological personality types. As my own research continued, we saw success practices exhibited in all standard classifications and it became increasingly apparent that *any* normal personality type can succeed. It also became clear that developing skills based on one's *own* personality makes synthesizing success habits much easier.

To initiate such learning patterns in the brain, I created *composite characters* from major personality types and interlaced the associated skills into stories so anyone can apply them, simply by being themselves, to gain what they want. Additionally, there are actionable success techniques sprinkled throughout, to make learning virtually effortless.

Naturally, how you manifest your American Dream will be different from those strategies you read about. Your success need not translate into material wealth, because being rich means only that you possess an abundant supply of something of value. Ultimately, it's up to you to define your success. And that's the beauty of an emotional IQ connection to your personality.

Whatever your situation today, this book will provide you with the knowledge of how to make your first million dollars, how to enhance your current financial wealth, or how to simply enjoy divine abundance in your life—all on your own terms.

An "I Can" Book

In essence, these pages will give you a sneak peek behind the curtain of what truly makes people successful, uncovering the mysteries of why average people do above-average things.

More than a how-to book, *Reawakening an American Dream* is an "I can" book that deconstructs success behaviors into common principles. It engages you to imagine or at least be thrilled by tales of adventure and adversity that fostered achievement.

Regard these as anyone-can-do-it stories—from a hitchhiker turned serial entrepreneur to a grandmother who made a fortune investing her cookie-jar money. You'll find each of them enlightening and instructive as they open doors to your own riches.

Experts with opinions on how to become rich come and go, and because their opinions are based on one single idea created through one person's filters, their very subjectivity increases the odds of failure for others. *The only expert capable of telling you how to create wealth is you.*

The truth is that no single formula for obtaining financial prosperity works, even though, all psychologically classified personalities share external traits. The missing secret is cerebral modifications that link behaviors to create wealth. Thus, making options for succeeding infinite.

As you journey through these chapters, you'll initiate a self-actualizing process to create new pathways in your brain, unlocking amazing personal power and permitting your individual outcomes to naturally unfold. Then your mind will be retooled for personal ways to prosper.

You also can gain new insight from your interpretations of Secret Success Standards throughout the book. These standards illustrate how individual and social behaviors of the characters translate into success.

Learning New Behaviors

In much the same way that children learn new behaviors because they are cognitively predisposed to learning, reading this book will unbridle abilities that free you to blaze paths that only you can truly see— that have always existed within you. When you choose to follow your natural instincts, others' beliefs won't hinder your journey, which makes yours simple and joyous.

Read these stories derived from the many millionaire study subjects from my behavioral-economic research. When you do, you are bound to see commonalities with yourself and understand how particular activities and decisions translate into wealth.

Use them to manufacture your own victory, regardless of your personality type.

No story in this book will fail to enlighten. You too can become rich. From these intimate stories, you'll realize that by connecting your personality to the vastness of your spirit, you have a prerogative to achieve your dream.

The Quiet Rich You'll Meet Here

In the chapters to come, you'll see what really makes people successful and how different people interpret their inherent connections. You'll meet the man who believed in love to such an extent that he wanted to bring that emotional bliss to as many people as possible. He made millions. You'll read about the boy who almost died on the Mexican-American border but prevailed against all odds and pursued his American Dream.

You'll also learn about a freckle-faced girl who grew up on a farm far away from any urban center. She learned self-respect and used it to overcome misfortune and abuse in the big city. You'll meet a man with bad luck and a broken neck who found his way off of a greasy factory floor into a life of wealth by using stamina and resolve.

A man ignored his handicap and found the power to do what he wanted and reaped great satisfaction. Another story features an African American boy who lost his parents and struggled to feel accepted. He rose to the top of his class and eventually to the top of his profession.

All of them illustrate the core concepts of the book and how they might apply to your life. These are the people who turned out to be more interesting, creative, and authentic than any of the pseudo-exciting wealthy people who fill the media spotlights. In addition, they earned every penny in unique and unpretentious ways.

These modest millionaires are true economic champions who never believed someone else should be shining their shoes.

Choose Your Own Pathway to Wealth

By learning about the heroes in this book, you might get the impression that achieving your dreams of wealth is easy. It's not. But it is *doable* if you take the entirety of these lessons to heart and assimilate them into your very being.

What's important, is to distinguish between what honors you and what does not. Know, that there are a whole group of Americans who possess respectable wealth but didn't buy in to the greed-is-good mentality. They disdain a get-rich-at-any-cost belief system.

Edged out of the spotlight by reality-show-style antics associated with accumulating wealth, they quietly honor themselves and their families by securing wealth with old-fashioned hard work and discipline.

Remember this: Each person is unique, and anyone can do what these heroes have done. That's the phenomenon that allows for endless pathways to achievement. More than that, it verifies all people can create customized activities that unleash the power to reach financial or personal victories.

The path of enrichment is realizing the interactive force within you and connecting it to your personality—that's your Financial Freedom Power Within!

So prepare to bear witness to the spiritual tenets at work in the marketplace. They will create financial miracles that bring the practitioners not only physical comforts but a serene soul that venerates what many good parents have taught their children.

CHAPTER 1

Roads to Riches

Archaeology is the only discipline that seeks to study human behavior and thought without having direct contact with either.
–Bruce G. Trigger

At the age of twenty-one, Thomas Seekins was a lone traveler from Boston who accepted situations as opportunities and turned them into affluence.

I met Thomas when we spent a week together on an archaeological dig in central Arizona. We were on a team of professional and avocational archaeologists uncovering and cataloging ancient history before a traffic interchange was built.

Thomas had moved with openness into the unknown—whether doing tedious labor or continuing his education. There was a carelessness in him that could have cursed his success, but he used it to go *around* obstacles rather than *through* them. He created momentum in a humble way that produced rewards larger than the Rocky Mountains.

As we worked side by side, Thomas shoveled back the layers of his own heritage and told me how he'd transformed a thin wallet into exceptional retirement wealth by letting things unfold around him.

* * *

Kneeling in a test trench, I would begin to experience all that Thomas Seekins had become, as we beheld one thousand years of ancient history. "Why did you go to Casa Grande before you went to Canada?" I asked, caring more about what I'd find in the ground then in my random shovel partner.

"There wasn't much in my backpack in those days,"

I stood up to shake the sifter's frame so I could get a better look at him.

"There was a lot of information in my soul about this place," he said.

Dust whipped around us as we fingered the rocks for pottery sherds. We were still in the topsoil—and still in the top layer of a friendship that started with curiosity about this man with jet-black hair and an angular face. "So, what was your secret, Thomas?"

"I was born in Boston, and my mom abandoned my dad and me. She moved out west somewhere when I was too young to remember her. Both of my parents had Native American genes. Dad never told me much about Mom. My dad's family was part of the Yavapai tribe. His great-grandfather had been shipped off the reservation to a school in Pennsylvania."

"Why would that happen?"

"To learn the ways of the white man, most likely. Please pass me the canteen. I'm scorched."

We took a water break as the morning sun rose. I rolled up the sleeves of my denim shirt. Thomas did the same with his starched white Brooks Brothers that had already collected soil stains. We both readjusted our Ray Bans.

"Time to shovel again. Maybe we'll uncover something," I said.

"My dad was from Boston, and he didn't like to focus too much on his past because he carried it with him all the time. Look, I have a dark complexion, dark eyes, dark hair. We didn't look like typical Bostonians. Dad did like to drink, and he played drums for a living. My life as a kid was lonely, and our little apartment didn't offer much in the way of a home life without my mom. I started working when I was twelve as a newspaper boy. Dad bought me a bicycle because my route was beyond walking distance from our apartment. I loved the job, especially collecting money from customers. Some of them let me step inside their stately homes when they went to get money to pay me. I had never seen anything like that before in my life."

As we continued to dig and sift, Thomas spoke incessantly. At lunch, we went our separate ways—he went to make some calls, and I took my lunch in the shade of a nearby Palo Verde tree. I recounted his story as I dosed off momentarily.

Thomas had no interest in music or musical theory unless there were practical applications. Growing up, he took on the role of guardian, organizing activities for him and his dad to fit a vision of the way things should have been. He knew how little control he had as the child of a single parent who was also an artist and an alcoholic. He took control where he could find it—as he did with the newspaper-delivery job.

He also learned to flow like a river when needed.

An observant child who didn't much like the life he was leading, Thomas continually imagined escaping into the homes where he delivered newspapers. He used all of his senses in concrete ways.

After saving a small amount of money, he told me he bid good-bye to his father late one summer. He wanted to see if he could feel any inherent connection to Arizona before fulfilling his dream of seeing the Canadian Rocky Mountains—a landscape he'd read about in school.

After lunch, we went back to digging. Thomas was silent, but I couldn't resist the urge to ask more about what propelled him through unknown lands.

"I knew so little about what was driving me," he explained. "All I did know was that I had some Native American heritage that made me feel as if I owned the land in a way that didn't involve money. This sense of ownership made me feel that I had to always do my best and honor all things."

He continued, "When I got to Calgary, the only job I could find was driving a taxi on the midnight-to-dawn shift. My boss gave me a map of the city, and I studied it by walking the streets when I wasn't driving. Fortunately, the riders were mostly inebriated and didn't put up too much of a fight when I lost the way.

"After I'd been driving for a year and a half, I got word that my dad had passed. He left me nothing—he'd been sick and had used up what little money he had. I was alone in the world. Being my best was now more important than ever."

As he spoke, I drifted into thoughts about how so many people suffer loneliness and despair. I sensed Thomas once felt desolation yet knew his life would progress. When I refocused, Thomas was talking about catching a ride to the train station so he could begin a new leg of the journey.

"I thanked the driver with a cup of coffee and doughnuts at the station café. As we were eating, he introduced me to a guy named Sam who was sweeping the floor. Perhaps he could get me a job in the station.

"What luck, right?

"Not really. The job didn't happen, but this was the first time I realized that there's a reason you meet everyone you do in life. Sam was a full-blooded Native American who had come to Canada in search of work. Like me, he had roots in the Southwest, but unlike me, he had studied them well—just on his own, out of personal interest.

"When we discovered we had something in common, he took me in for a few days and let me live in his little place. When he got off his shift, he told me stories about my ancestors and what they had gone through as a race, how they suffered from white man's diseases, displacement, murder, and how they'd become prisoners on their own land."

Thomas explained it was Sam's kindness and knowledge that allowed a new attitude to settle into his mind. I could see at that moment a humble warrior behind his dark eyes.

Beads of sweat gathered on Thomas's wrinkled brow and rolled down his face, mixing with fine dirt in the wind from the digging. Without flinching, he continued.

"Sam showed me how to envision myself as a seeker of knowledge through a willingness to work hard and pay attention. He said he'd heard there was a need for workers at a resort to the west. After a week with Sam, I said good-bye and finally boarded that train to Jasper on the promise of finding work. It was the last I ever heard from Sam."

Thomas tried to wipe a tear from his eye without me seeing. Then he swiftly filled his chest with breath. "I felt unsure of my belief in the person I had been. Sam helped me identify that at least I was on the right track in wanting to be a responsible, respectful person and a worker dedicated to doing a good job."

The constant digging and sifting allowed me to think as I listened to this man's story. It was mid-July when Thomas had stepped off the train in Jasper. It was hot, hotter than he'd expected. In my mind, I was on the journey with him—moving on that train as he passed through the vast wilderness and anonymous towns.

I could feel that same heat from the sun above me as he talked about spending the night in a shabby motel with only forty dollars in his pocket but a dream the size of Canada in his heart. Although he was full of hope and his will to work had the power of youthful enthusiasm, he was an immigrant in this unfamiliar country.

"It was at a gray, heartless-looking building that I acquired the legal right to work in Canada," Thomas explained.

"I filled out the paperwork and eventually found my way to the desk of a clerk tasked with job placement assistance. The clerk said, 'You've heard of a job possibility, but you don't have the job, eh? Well, let's look at the newspaper ads.' He skimmed through the paper handed it back to me and said, 'Maybe tomorrow.'"

I pushed my shovel into the pile of dirt we'd created. "That sounds rather useless. What did you do?"

"I read the ads myself! One of them was from a company looking for an experienced welder. So I walked out of the office, went to a pay phone, called the company, explained my situation to the owner, and said, 'I'd like to come on down and just talk with you. And if there's anything I can do, we'll see how it works out.'"

"That was courageous. What did he say?"

"When I met him the next day, I was dressed in my best clothes, even though the welding shop was a squat, dirty building in the middle of nowhere. A man with the build of a linebacker greeted me. He didn't smile, but his eyes reflected a kindness that reassured me. 'You here for the job?' he asked. I said, indeed I was.

"Then he said to me, 'You have no experience, yet you said I should give you a chance. Have you ever held a welding torch?' I said no but that I'd seen one being used and I was willing to learn. If he could take the time to train me, I'd be the best worker he'd ever hired.

"He agreed to give me a couple of hours in the welding shop to show how fast I'd learn. Sure enough, I found my first job in Canada."

> **I was strong and willing to learn. If he could take the time to train me, I'd be the best worker he'd ever hired.**

The afternoon sun now cast a shadow in the pit where we'd been digging, but Thomas had been talking with the same enthusiasm he had after his morning coffee.

"How did you live before you got paid?" I asked, wiping my cheek.

"After one night in the motel, I went to the owner of the motel and said, 'I'm new in town, and I just got hired. If you'll allow me to stay in my room until my first paycheck arrives, I'll clean and do maintenance for you after work each day. Just give me a list of chores.' The lady who owned the place wrote out a list on the spot."

"You landed on your feet twice in one day!"

"Yes, and it taught me a lesson that I'd never learned in school. It isn't enough to *see* a chance; one has to *take* the chance."

It occurred to me that Thomas was on the road to success because he focused his effort in any situation. By doing this, he pushed his best qualities to the surface and integrated interpersonal skills that were easily recognized by others—especially those who might partner with him for economic gain.

By now, we had sifted a few potsherds out of the dirt, and Thomas was examining them with a magnifying glass. "Just think of the hands that must have held this so many years ago. How old do you think it is? Who do you think held this, and what did they think about their life?"

My interest was shifting from the past to the present. "Some men's curiosity runs deep, Thomas. I'll bet your curiosity helped you make your way through life."

"Sure, I guess it did. Do you want me to keep telling you how I got here? You're a curious man too, and we've still got hours of daylight."

"Yes," I replied with some fatigue. "Later, when I drift off to sleep after this exhausting day, thinking about your story will help me sleep peacefully."

> **Thomas was always ready to move forward, try something new, and in everything he did, he was certain to do his best no matter what.**

Thomas did well at the welding job but eventually found that it did not fulfill him in any meaningful way. In November that year, he also enrolled in a work-study program hoping to bolster his ability with numbers. When he told me the best thing about his school experience was meeting a young woman named Sally, I knew his story had taken a turn.

They shared a wonderful relationship, but Sally soon gave him an ultimatum: choose to settle down or leave her alone. Instead of staying rooted in his comfort zone with Sally and study accounting, he contemplated his next move.

Open to his next adventure being better than his last one, Thomas went downtown and stepped into his next job.

"I walked into a local bar in Jasper to meet a friend. It wasn't the cleanest place, but the guys were friendly. I'd had a couple of beers and one of them said, 'If you want a job, go to the dock on Nancy Lake and ask for Bill. He'll fly you into my fishing camp, and you can work for me.' The camp was on a beautiful island two-hundred and fifty miles northeast of Winnipeg."

"Thomas, most people don't experience that much luck."

"Luck?" He winced. "It's not luck; it's seeing opportunity. If you look at your own life, you'll probably find a few experiences like this yourself!"

He was right, but I was more interested in his life than mine, so I placed my spade into the leather side holster and listened.

"In those days," Thomas continued, "roads in that area were mostly dirt, making the prospect of getting a ride remote. But eventually, out of a cloud of smoke from a passing tractor-trailer appeared an old pickup truck that swerved to a stop. I got in and began a new journey that included a cast of characters and a variety of rides."

Pulling off his sunglasses and wiping them with a dirty bandana, he looked to the ground. Then he continued his story.

"After four long days of driving on back roads, I arrived— walked right to the dock and found Bill, a total stranger. I had no idea what the conditions would be, but I put my life in his hands. No one lives without fear; all great warriors experience it but overcome it by accessing their courage. Not many people get the chance to do that.

"Together, we flew north to the fishing camp in a single-engine Cessna with homemade pontoons. When we landed, the camp was deserted.

"Bill and I opened the camp ourselves. We got the generator going, hooked up all the plumbing, and took the plywood off the windows. Other workers arrived daily, and within a week, we were ready to host wealthy American fishermen," Thomas recalled.

Over the next eight weeks, Thomas took guests fishing, polished boats, and hauled luggage.

"We cooked their meals, fixed tents, did *everything* for them," he said. "And to make things more difficult, while the guests slept inside, the guides had to sleep outdoors."

> No one lives without fear; all great warriors experience it but overcome it by accessing their courage.

As the sun painted the desert early evening orange, the dinner bell rang. Our group was served a communal meal on picnic tables at the dig site. Thomas sat next to me, and I needed to hear more. "You must have loved that fishing camp experience," I said, my curiosity piqued. "What was next?"

"The season came to an end in late September, and I stayed to close down the camp. One of the guests had offered me an opportunity to work in Panama during the off-season. So, it was back down that dusty road again with my thumb and backpack. I had no idea who I really was or where I was going at that point in my life.

"With perfect timing, the weather turned cold, and I was going to Central America. On the way past Calgary, it started snowing—hard. I had gotten a ride with a hunter who was going to Jasper, so I decided to stay warm and take the ride back to a familiar place."

Thomas talked throughout dinner about how the area around Jasper resonated with his soul.

Jasper had been a fur-trading outpost established in 1813. It was accessible from Edmonton, the capital of Alberta, and close to the scenic Icefields Parkway that connected the city to the resort town of Banff. It sounded to me like its natural, rustic beauty mirrored Thomas's soul—a diamond in the rough.

Located in Athabasca River Valley at the confluence of the Miette River, Jasper became the convergence of his heart, soul, and mind—and the place he'd become successful in obtaining riches far greater than those earned by the legendary fur trade. I wasn't surprised he returned to Jasper.

> **It sounded to me like its natural, rustic beauty mirrored Thomas's soul—a diamond in the rough.**

Thomas patted his belly, full from supper. "When we came to the motel north of the city near Pyramid Lake, it was snowing hard, and I had my choice of any room in the place. The next day, after the snow had stopped, I woke up, put on my coat, and stepped outside to see trees covered in thick, white snow that looked as if it had moved in to be a permanent resident.

"The tranquility of the landscape was interrupted by the smell of frying bacon. I followed my nose to the kitchen. There, I met the motel owner and two women—one middle-aged and white, the other older and darker with a big round face framing her hearty smile. By that evening, I had once again agreed to do odd jobs in exchange for a room. By the end of the winter season, I had also become the front-desk clerk."

He mused for a moment and said, "You know, I felt as if I owned the place!"

By now most of the archaeological team was leaving the table. The air hinted of a chill. Campfire aroma mixed with light-hearted laughter in the distance, but I was still digging to unearth relics burred deep in the layers of this man's life.

Thomas rubbed his index finger and thumb together in a circular motion as if he had found a piece of unwashed dirt as he continued.

"When my lifeforce beckoned, I left that remote motel in the woods and found my *chi* driving a taxi in the heart of Jasper. I drove a cab long enough to meet a man named Harry who owned a hotel not far from the center of town."

"When Harry got in my cab, we talked the whole way about all the work I had done. When he handed me the tip, I refused it and said, 'I'm looking for a better job. If you hear of anything, that would be the best tip of all.' Within two weeks, I was working at the coffeehouse in Harry's hotel."

"It seems like you can smell opportunity like a cup of hot coffee, Thomas!" I laughed.

"No kidding! Harry had no children and was hoping to retire but couldn't face the prospect of selling the business he'd started from scratch. Once I got the job at the coffeehouse, I worked more than full time for Harry.

"I liked him—we had a bond. That winter was a bad one, and we needed to put up scaffolding to repair damage to windows. A tough job, but I came through and got it done. It made Harry happy, although there were times he worried for my safety. He was one of those souls who made it possible for me to be here today talking with you and searching for ancient possessions that my people left behind."

"You were like Harry's son. Did he leave the hotel to you in his will?" I joked.

"Oh no, that would be luck, and I never count on that!"

"Sounds like the story is about to get better," I said, rubbing my hands together and wishing for a sweater to keep out the cool night air.

Thomas rubbed his hands in agreement and continued. "What came next was my first challenge to lead. My new role came with higher accountability and effort than I'd ever known. It required even harder work and further adaptation of my values. It put me in a no-place-to-hide spotlight while forcing me to strengthen my belief in truth and competitive fair play. I continued my desire to be the best at everything I undertook. Three and a half years later, I was asked to buy the hotel."

"Did you?"

"I bandied about the pros and cons in my head for days. A feeling akin to hunger lingered in the pit of my stomach although I lacked appetite. How many scenarios would I think of before I could make a decision? With each new thought, I became fearful that one never knows what will happen in the future.

"Then, as if in a sign, a mild breeze swept into my room and gave me a feeling that I deciphered as, *Take the step that is before you now. Believe in your ability to survive, and the next steps will follow.* In that instant, I decided to buy Harry's business and see what would happen. I signed a note to pay Harry a down payment of thirty thousand dollars directly from money I earned by increasing the hotel's revenue, with further terms to be discussed."

> **Take the step that is before you now. Believe in your ability to survive, and the next steps will follow.**

"That was brave and bold! Didn't you have any backing?"

"No. And I didn't know anything about the process called due diligence. I quickly found out Harry didn't have much of a business. It had negative equity because of the large mortgage held by the local bank. His various lines of credit were being used to pay employees. Harry faced top-line revenue problems due to increased competition from newer hotels. And the leasing agreements on most of the equipment were in arrears, with other accounts receivable long overdue.

"The only asset Harry had on the balance sheet was goodwill—well, and I guess me. Harry intended no malice in offering me a chance to share in a company on the brink of bankruptcy. He simply couldn't accept the idea of walking away from something he worked so hard to grow."

Thomas told me how news of the partnership spread fast, thanks to gossip. People saw a man who was like a son to Harry take hold of a handicapped situation and manage the limited resources.

At the time, the year-round population was small, making Thomas quite visible. It also gave him a distinct advantage in implementing his plan. After a long recession, the city of Calgary, a major metropolitan area close to Jasper, was becoming the hub of the Canadian oil industry. Thomas knew that, with his instincts, he could benefit from this macroeconomic event.

"You're an astute man," I said. "Did you learn this in accounting school?" I was interested to know why some people connect the dots and others miss all the clues.

"Not really. I just paid attention. The Jasper population typically increases fourfold during peak summer visiting periods. The opposite happens in winter. Tourists disappear from the town in direct proportion to the amount of snow. Business freezes over as well, but I used that first winter as a co-owner of Harry's hotel to incubate a plan. I knew that for the hotel to be a successful endeavor, it had to be managed with cunning. I spent long hours poring over all of the challenges and possibilities until one morning, the lightbulb turned on.

"I could offer a three-day-stay package complete with transportation, food, lodging, and activities at a better price than anyone from miles around. The resort would be filled every weekend, and I didn't need to count on longer-stay customers from far away."

Thomas was not an anxious man. He moved slowly but precisely, thinking through one thing at a time. As I watched his hands artistically move through the air while he spoke, it occurred to me that his soul was uniquely connected with his personality.

Perhaps subconsciously, he recognized practical concerns and put them into an instinctual understanding by applying new perspectives to routine business. What he was describing about his life showed simple belief in himself that gave him clarity and helped him expand his skillset.

My mind raced as we scraped the bowls once filled with ice cream and prickly pear syrup. The night sky had become brilliant, as if every star in the heavens came out to hear this story.

> **It occurred to me that Thomas's soul was uniquely connected with his personality.**

Thomas was older than me, but I was the one getting tired. When I was about to suggest we call it a night, he made a shivering sound and continued.

"They were cold, lonely nights that winter! I spent most of them by the fire researching other businesses in Jasper. I examined the strengths, weaknesses, opportunities, and threats from as many perspectives as I could. I isolated all the services that might appeal to the target demographic and pinpointed friends in town who provided them.

"Then I called all of them to suggest we form a coalition. Every member would be one of a kind—that is, one would be a shuttle service, one a rental shop, one a fishing store, and so on down the list. Together, our services totaled all the things needed for the perfect vacation weekend. From there, I created full-package programs for every possible style of weekend tourist.

"The coalition businesses marshaled their resources and worked as a team sharing planning, marketing, and administrative duties. By functioning as a hospitality group and focusing on one market—Calgary residents only—their money, resources, and effectiveness provided exponential benefits. By spring, we unrolled a campaign unlike any the town had ever seen. That summer was the best business season the town had ever had, and Harry's hotel generated more revenue than at any time in its history.

"This pattern continued over the next several years as our hospitality group became obsessed with innovation. In effect, we turned a sleepy town into a destination dynamo."

Astonished and no longer fatigued, I exclaimed, "You did it simply by doing something entirely different, knowing it required being flexible and taking a chance."

"Yes, but more was going on behind the scenes," he added. "Back at the hotel, I was doing my own financial engineering and negotiating receivables. I even fired some deadwood employees. The hotel finally had a positive cash flow, expanding its profit margins, and I could start addressing debt.

"I too was making more money than I'd ever dreamed and became known as the man who made the town come alive. The enormity of my new reality was mind-boggling, but I continued to face the challenges head on, one step at a time."

> I became known as the man
> who made the town come alive.

Thomas continued, "The town quickly evolved. We renovated Harry's hotel and occupancy rates climbed. Soon, the biggest hotels in the area took notice—even the mountain's most lucrative hotel, owned by a large corporation in Toronto. The rumor was that the owners wanted to remain number one, and they intended to take me down a notch. They weren't gonna let their MBA bosses from big universities get smoked by some guy like me." Thomas grinned.

"Late one afternoon, I received a call from a shuttle driver in town alerting me that a Toronto 'suit' was in Jasper for a big meeting at their best property. Sure enough, a week later, I received a call to meet with that hotel's managing director.

"We met for two hours, and when I drove home, I still couldn't believe what I'd heard. The corporation wanted to buy my hotel but didn't want to pay me. They wanted to pay off the first-position bank loan and close down our hotel."

"Unbelievable! What did you do?"

"The feeling of being disrespected kicked my thinking skills into high gear. I headed down to the bank that held the loan. It was a Friday afternoon. I walked in and requested to talk to the manager. He was very busy. When I insisted on an appointment, he finally invited me to his home.

"That evening, I brought a six-pack of beer, and we sat around his coffee table talking until almost midnight. Finally, the banker said, 'I've seen you around for years and you've faithfully worked hard. I'll delay the sell on the past-due note if you can show me what you can do.'"

"An ace in the hole," I sighed, as if sitting in the stands of a prize fight.

"Yes, and I was ready to implement. The following Monday, I flew to Toronto determined to meet the executives who threatened to end my world. In the meeting, I startled those conceited corporate types when I told them my plan was to be the number-one resort hotel in the area. After they caught their collective breath, I proposed a partnership if they were agreeable to maintaining my standards."

At that moment, I could see majesty in the eyes of this simple man who had knelt beside me all day digging in the dirt. It was clear I too was beginning to feel empowered.

"The top brass around the table looked out the side of their eyes at each other but then on me when I said we'd now discuss the hotel's current assets and liabilities. Then I told them, 'Next, you can tell me what you can bring to the table. If I feel your people can exceed current expectations, then I will sign a letter of intent stating that if you keep all the salaried workers, you can keep any profits after the five-hundred-thousand-dollar bank loan is paid down. Then I'll increase your percentage of ownership, and once Harry is dead, you will have a controlling interest to do what you want with the hotel.' By the end of that day, I had an agreement from one of the largest hospitality corporations in Canada."

Hearing about this knockout punch, I praised him. "The balance of inherent wisdom and discipline gave you ownership of your destiny and opened the road to your success."

> **It was his balance of inherent wisdom and discipline that gave him ownership of his destiny and opened the road to his success.**

"Yes, in my travels I was accustomed to letting things be, even in the face of unfairness. But I also knew when to push my limits and face the enemy. I was able to keep the hotel open until Harry's death—a bridge crossed, not burned—and that bridge connected me to my first million dollars.

"You can call it being impetuous or call it taking a risk. But making a quick decision to jump on the plane to Toronto wasn't a random incident. Rather, it came as a result of consistently executed actions like a wound clock spring."

I shared what I was feelings with him. "Thomas, I'm profoundly moved. Personal power does not come by chance. Rather, it comes as a rational process of fusing learned experiences to support a focused cause."

"Thanks for your astute observations, Kevin."

But I was still curious about how he filled his wallet and since we had, by now, such a strong bond, I simply asked him straightway. Thomas was more than happy to share.

He brushed off his dirty sleeve as if he were preparing to make a speech. Then he looked up toward the moon and said, "Within two years of signing the letter of intent, the Toronto company asked me to be an advisor for other properties it owned for a handsome salary and a piece of equity bonus. Harry was prouder of me than he was about saving his hotel. Four years later he died…I think because he finally had peace.

"Several weeks after Harry's death, I was meeting with the company CFO, who had become my friend. In passing, he said he'd never seen anybody create net worth as conscientiously as me. I asked if he knew how much that was, because I'd never stopped to count. 'Six million, roughly,' the CFO replied.

"I hadn't seen that one coming."

> **It came as a result of consistently executed actions that wound my momentum like a clock spring.**

Our first day on the dig ended around 11:00 p.m. with both of us finally out of steam. We said good night.

The next morning at breakfast, Thomas told me that on the way to his tent, his mind drifted back to thoughts of Sam in the train station. He thanked me for helping him remember.

By the end of our archaeology experience that week, we had unearthed new artifacts and the promise of an improved understanding about ancient times. I had also gained a new friend in Thomas, and we kept in touch.

Today, still a humble warrior, he spends time on Native American reservations teaching and inspiring those who advocate for economic advancement. He constantly encourages people of color not to be afraid to open doors and find affluence.

In the end, life worked out well for this free-spirited traveler turned multimillionaire. Thomas moved into the top 1% of wealth not only because of his personal essence and hard work but because of his momentum-creating philosophy to collaborate for the benefit all.

In my last journal entry from the dig, I included a quote from Thomas to live among the artifacts. "You may not always see the end of the road but go down there and check it out. Be yourself, enjoy the ride, and do the best you can. Something good always comes out of that."

You too can use Secret Success Standards from Thomas's life story like the one's below, as stepping-stones to your own accomplishments:

- Embrace the unknown with enjoyment and let momentum lead you into a world of affluence.
- Release yourself from others' expectations; view events without judgment.
- Push your best qualities to the surface and integrate them with your interpersonal skills so others can easily recognize them.

CHAPTER 2

Broke Not Broken

However bad life may seem, there is always something you can do
and succeed at. Where there's life, there's hope.
– **Stephen Hawking**

In the 1990s, one of my corporate directives was to expand my firm's strategic revenue model into markets that had growing demographics. After several months of running hypotheticals, my first stop was Colorado. The fresh mountain air helped make my ongoing assignment of developing investment policies more agreeable.

Andy and Sarah, who lived down the road from the house I'd rented, had their own ongoing mission; they were raising a son who had suffered an unusual childhood accident. At the time we met, Shaun was a senior in high school and well-intentioned adults were encouraging him to seek support in managing his disability. However, he didn't view himself as having limitations. Instead, he devoted himself to projects that would increase his purpose and enhance his confidence.

After high school, Shaun left the safety of that Colorado town to follow his American dream. I departed soon after, but we stayed in touch. Shaun's amazing story of uniqueness began to unfold as a story via my digital devices.

As the years passed, I witnessed him overcoming stigmas to find work. I prayed when his diversity caused him risks and cheered when he overcame barriers. For him, inclusion was never a question.

Shaun never felt his uniqueness was anything less than an advantage to him as he focused his best attributes toward the success he dreamed about. In so doing, there blossomed a power and supremacy that came from accepting who he was.

Eventually, Shaun fell in love, raised his own family, and attained the dream of financial freedom he had always held deep in his heart.

* * *

It was a Sunday when I took possession of the rented home where I would spend the following six months. It didn't take long to settle in, and as I shoveled light snowdrifts off the porch, a man, a woman, and a boy arrived with a plate of cookies, a short stack of foam cups, and a covered silver pitcher.

"We're the Simons," the man said. "I'm Andy, and this is Sarah and Shaun. We saw you come in today and wanted to give you a welcome. You must be renting from John Moser."

"Hello. Yes," I said. "I'll be your neighbor while I work on a project. This place offers the kind of quiet beauty I need right now."

Shaun spoke up. "I made the hot chocolate. Mom made the cookies." Sarah held out the tray as Shaun grabbed the pitcher—and that was when I noticed his prosthetic hand. "Please, come in," I said.

"Thanks," Sarah replied as I held open the front door. "If you need any household stuff, let me know. We have plenty extra."

"Thanks for the welcome," I said as Sarah set out the refreshments. "I'll be a quiet neighbor, but if I can help you, my door is open."

Shaun, an enterprising boy, grabbed the placemats piled on a box in the kitchen and set them on the table. "I know you saw my hand," he said with quiet dignity. "I don't like people to feel uncomfortable, so I'm happy to tell you the story."

I was taken aback but immensely curious about this open and captivating boy.

"Do you want to know what happened? We might as well get it over with now," Shaun announced.

> **I was taken aback but immensely curious about this open and captivating boy.**

"Shaun was ten when his curiosity took him away from home one day," Sarah abruptly added.

"Let me tell the story, Mom!"

"Let me say Shaun has a fascination with mechanics," Sarah explained. "That starts the story, son."

"Okay, Mom," Shaun responded, eager to talk without offending his mother.

"Well, anyway, when I was little, I loved to watch my dad fix our car and everything else. Once, I took apart Mom's vacuum cleaner and didn't get it back together until the carpet got too filthy. I got grounded until I restored it to the way I found it. Vacuuming became my chore from that day on."

Andy broke in almost to protect his son from reliving the words. "There's a wood-processing plant down by the river. I worked there a few days a week as a second job. Once in a while when Shaun got home from school, he'd walk down there to meet me and watch workers maneuver the heavy machinery and lumber. The economy wasn't that great and some of the shifts were pretty slow. On one of the days I wasn't working, Shaun went there without me, and that was the day he had the accident."

Shaun piped in. "I couldn't figure it out; hardly anyone was on the factory floor that day. I walked over to my favorite machine, the horizontal resaw—it was small, compact, and only as high as my shoulder. I loved watching the spiked rollers chip through lumber with a slow grinding sound. It wasn't running, but the wood was fed into it and ready to go. I couldn't help but punch the small green button.

"And that's when it happened."

Nervously Andy began glancing at his wife. Rather than engaging, she attended to the hot chocolate with even greater determination.

Visibly upset, Andy took over again in a softer voice as if to shield his words. "When the sound of the saw echoed in the empty plant, a few men who'd been in the foreman's office rushed in. But they were too late to pull my boy away. By the time the machine was stopped, it had cut away Shaun's hand."

Speaking louder, he concluded, "Thanks to the men's fast action, an ambulance soon arrived, and Shaun was in surgery within a half hour."

"I didn't even feel it," Shaun added casually. "It was like watching a movie."

"You were in shock," Sarah consoled, finally able to join the conversation. "As his mom, I'm still in shock, but Shaun adapted. He only cried once, and that was when he saw my concern for him."

"But I did struggle with it, Mom. I just didn't let you see that part."

I had intended to ask privately about the impact of this injury on the family when Andy jumped in with renewed confidence and more details. "Shaun's recovery was difficult. He had a hard time with the new prosthetic hand and felt guilty for having done something wrong."

"Every night," Sarah said in her comforting way, "Andy and I reminded Shaun that no matter what, he was resilient, and his ability to adapt and bounce back would make him stronger than other people. I had to tell myself that, too, especially when I prayed."

Shaun continued, "I was just a kid, and I realized that the favorite things on my shelf and in my yard—motorcycles, airplanes, electronic games, my bike—all required some kind of mechanical handling that I couldn't perform with one hand. I felt angry, then sad, but I knew that there must be a way around it."

> **I felt angry, then sad, but I knew that there must be a way around it.**

He then stepped into the center of the kitchen as if he walked on stage. "My mom and dad, if you can't already tell, are good people who gave me the intuitional fortitude to combat the hopelessness I sometimes let myself feel.

"Since the age of ten, I've had a series of prosthetic hands, each one better than the last. I always have something new to look forward to, and I'm gaining new experiences and a bit more dexterity with each new fake hand. How many other people can say that about their real right hands?"

The four of us moved into the dining room and devoured all of the cookies and hot cocoa. We continued to talk for almost an hour and I learned from my new neighbors all about Shaun's life after the accident.

I quickly recognized that Shaun needed to have passion for something that would bolster his emotional resilience and allow him to adapt to his prosthetic hand. He was blessed to have parents who did exactly that to keep him occupied, happy, and thinking about things beyond himself.

> **Shaun needed to have a passion for something that would bolster his emotional resilience and allow him to adapt to his prosthetic hand and think about things beyond himself.**

Andy, a religious man, also spent time in conversation with Shaun about following in his footsteps and becoming a devoted Christian. Andy talked about how physical joys were important but only as they aided in the path to Heaven. His aim was for Shaun to dedicate himself to God's will, so he wouldn't feel hurt when the lack of a natural physical ability prevented some of his dreams from coming true.

However, like most kids, Shaun was not completely sold on the idea and wanted nothing to do with his dad's approach to life. Seeing this, Andy astutely adopted a new tactic.

One night over the usual family dinner together, Andy announced it was time for Shaun to practice driving the family car—after Shaun met a few conditions. The church pastor had agreed to give Andy a nonworking 1942 Oldsmobile, and if Shaun could make it run, it would be his free and clear.

The house had only been mine for a short time but as I sat there with this family and watched father and son re-create that fascinating experience, it was quickly becoming my warm, safe place.

With a glimpse of childhood innocence in his voice, Shaun said, "I was thrilled to have a car we could work on, and I asked Dad, 'Do I have to wait until the car is fixed to drive?'"

Andy added with clear recollection. "I said, 'No. If you work on the car with me every day and we make good progress, I'll take you out to Old Creek Road, hand you the keys to my car and sit right next to you as you practice driving. Then by the time you get your license, you'll know how to drive the Olds.'"

Shaun kept his part of the deal! Every day after school, he worked in the heated garage handing tools to his dad. At first, his prosthesis frustrated him as he'd fumble and drop tools into the engine area. Andy made him bend in to fish them out, but as Shaun did so, he would teach his son about an engine part. Shaun caught on and rarely complained.

If he had trouble, he worked to figure it out on his own, or he asked Andy for help.

I could easily see that father and son were good at collaboration. It was fun to listen to Shaun talk about finally, at age fourteen, he was able to start his driving adventures sitting next to Andy in the family car.

Shaun discovered he was as excited to work on the 1942 Oldsmobile as he was to drive his dad's car for the first time. He told me it dawned on him that even if the classic cruiser convertible wasn't fully functioning, it held the promise of beauty, style, and performance—much like him.

He also saw his own future brightly unfolding.

> Even if the classic cruiser convertible wasn't fully functioning, it held the promise of beauty, style, and performance— much like him.

During that time, Andy was overjoyed to see his son's dedication. It took father and son two years to get the Oldsmobile running. Often, they waited for weeks after ordering hard-to-get parts. Although they took breaks for holidays and for Shaun's school exams, they both remained eternally loyal to the project.

Andy told me that the process of restoring the car caused Shaun to treat all those around him with greater sincerity and fairness— showing no sign of being distracted, embarrassed, or limited by his disability. Although he didn't always accept conventional rules, he faithfully followed all the mechanical guidelines from his dad.

When he turned sixteen, Shaun's reward was owning the best-looking, sharpest automobile in town. A classic Olds 98 with cream-colored body and red detailing, sitting on fat black tires around sixteen-inch chrome pancake hubs.

Shaun was excited to add, "I was the only one of my friends who knew how to drive a car before I was sixteen and was the only one who *had* a car."

After we all had a good laugh Shaun said. "The last year and a half of high school was great. That car helped me win friends and honored my mechanical hand. I did things that were impossible with my other hand, like pop off bottle caps and pull hockey pucks from the ice-cold lake. It's like a wrench I never have to put down!"

As the joviality subsided and we all got up to leave the table, Shaun fell back on his right foot with momentarily childlike consideration. "Hey Kevin, will you come to my graduation?"

Finding it hard to resist his sincerity, I agreed as long as he would drive me there.

He approved, and I took an empty sip of my long-gone hot chocolate. Looking over at me with the same sincerity I recognized in her son's eyes, Sarah offered to go back home and prepare dinner for all of us.

As soon as the door closed behind Sarah, Andy pivoted back to me. He was ready to burst with more of Shaun's story. I could feel his pride, but the scars he carried from a painful parenthood were not far from the surface. I suggested we sit on the couch in the other room. As we walked, Andy began to speak.

"Although Shaun accepted that he was different, he never accepted limitations. That's where I think he discovered the power of not judging himself. He learned to trust that he could adapt with dignity to any insult thrown his way. He knew this because in overcoming his suffering, he had established peace with who he was and what he was capable of achieving."

As we sat with our shoes off, I saw that Shaun was listening to his father speak about him with the same suspect any teenager would have. "Thanks, Dad," he said. "I also have good friends."

"Tell me about them," I said, turning my attention exclusively to him.

"Steve and Victor! I've known them since the first grade. But Steve's going off to college after we graduate. Victor's not going to leave; he can't afford college."

"What are your plans for college?"

"I've already been accepted into an electronics trade school that's about twenty-five miles from here. I got a scholarship because of my hand but my grades were good, too." I noticed no remorse in his voice and, over time, came to recognize the resolve that powered this special person.

> I noticed no remorse in his voice and, over time, came to recognize the resolve that powered this special person.

Dinner that night was exactly what I needed to feel better about my move north. Thankfully for me, it led to many other invitations that I reciprocated during my time living there.

I attended Shaun's high school graduation and gave him voice-to-text software as a gift. I asked him to keep in touch with me in emails that he could speak instead of type. He sent me a hand-written thank-you note that included his email address. I remember wondering at that time if he would be running a stock brokerage office for me some day.

Through our emails to come, I learned that Shaun had excelled at the two-year trade school program and graduated ahead of schedule. He then took a job with a radio-tower-operations company, driving to remote broadcasting tower locations in a four-wheel drive with the chief engineer to assist in checking or repairing transmitters. He loved the freedom, the long drives over rough terrain, and the smell of tiny transmitter huts powered day and night by megavolts of electric power.

On one slow day in the office, Shaun got a call from his friend Victor, who told him that someone couldn't pay a repair bill and had left behind a 1956 Chevy at his gas station. The two friends spent the next four weekends fixing it so they could sell it. After it was running, washed, and waxed, it took only three days to sell. Shaun wrote to me that it was the easiest money he'd ever made. I knew fixing and selling that Chevy was fun because he was collaborating with someone he cared about. It was a big milestone in his life.

Shortly after the car sold, he was promoted at work and relocated to his company's corporate office in Colorado Springs. There, he moved into an apartment and for the first time, was managing money on his own. Twice a month, he'd cash his paycheck and put money in separate envelopes to budget for bills. He never had much left to spend on socializing, but he managed to go to a happy hour every Friday at a nearby restaurant frequented by young locals.

Some of Shaun's new friends were curious about his prosthetic hand, yet his confidence talking about it never wavered. However, when it came to dating, he faced questions even Superman couldn't answer. For Shaun, romance required a whole new set of skills that certainly doesn't come easy for most men. His natural charm made him pleasant to be around, but he was happiest doing tasks alone that required detailed logistics and technical skills. Women somehow didn't seem logical to him.

After a few awkward dates, he became confused about how to get to know a woman from work he was attracted to. For the first time, he was realizing how someone else might provide the completeness in life that he desired.

I enjoyed hearing from him during that time on his path of meeting, knowing, and loving his future wife, Judith. I enjoyed it so much that I saved his email to this day. Here is a portion of it:

I met Judith while on a routine tech check. As the traffic person, she's a vital link in coordinating on-air activities. Her job requires skills to keep information scheduled throughout the broadcast day—and she makes her job look easy. She's smart and beautiful—and she talked to me first!

Over the course of a year, I received similar emails from Shaun about his relationship with Judith. He was puzzled about how opposites could attract—he was on the shy side while she was outgoing and had many friends. I gave him advice to the best of my ability, which might not be saying much. Yet before long, Judith became his partner in life and in business. The two were opposites, but Shaun and Judith were devoted to making it work.

After a small civil wedding, they moved into Judith's home. With two incomes and one home, they were enjoying each other and having fun. Shaun confided in me that he wanted to have children, but Judith was reluctant about starting a family. He wrote that she was his muse and he was doing well in his career because of her support—but wanted to have a child to rear just as he was by Andy and Sarah.

Several months went by without any communication from Shaun. Then I heard they'd decided to put aside any desire for having a family because Judith wanted them to accumulate more money. Shaun appeared okay with the idea, but I could sense mixed emotions, so I called him.

"How's it going, Shaun?"

"Good, Kev, but I have to tell you that in the months when I wasn't writing, I was going to self-help seminars hoping to find my way through some struggles. They fell short because I didn't need soup. I needed meat and potatoes that a spoon—or maybe even a mechanical hand—could stand up in.

"One weekend, I went to Denver to attend a motivational seminar that Mom and Dad paid for, and I felt like I was on a quiz show or at a circus. It caused me to feel good for about a week, but nothing in me changed. I realized that people cannot hug their way to success and happiness.

"You know, everyone but me notices my prosthetic. I am so over being labeled 'handicapped,' because the only real limitations are in the mind. You probably know what I mean."

At that moment it struck me how much Shaun had grown since leaving his sleepy hometown for a more competitive environment.

> **It struck me how much Shaun had grown since leaving his sleepy hometown for a more competitive environment.**

It was rare for us to talk by phone, and I didn't want any awkward silence, so I responded with the first thing that came to mind. "My friend went to one of those seminars once. It cost as much money as she made in a month. There was even a life-size cutout of the presenter the audience could pose with. Of course, the *real guy* had pictures of himself with *real* presidents and *real* movie stars. What she learned was that bold people get rich. She liked that because she already was bold. But when I asked her, 'What do all the people who aren't bold do?' she got miffed."

This time, Shaun was the one on the verge of awkward silence, so I graciously continued. "You've heard me say the only way to become successful is not by copying how someone else did it but by using the gifts only you have. It sounds to me that you learned to listen to the sound of your soul."

We had a long and wonderful conversation that day. We laughed, shared, and contemplated. Shaun seemed to have found something he was looking for his whole life. I was not surprised there was no more contact for almost two years. Then one day in the U.S. mail, I received a birth announcement that said: "We are blessed to announce Robert Benjamin Simons has been born into our lives".

Coincidentally it was on the same date in January that I'd met Shaun, Andy, and Sarah, so I felt doubly blessed.

I immediately sent a gift for the baby—a check to start baby Robert's college fund—and got a thoughtful handwritten thank-you note in return a few weeks later.

Several months quickly passed, and I received Shaun's email about how wonderful life was, how well the baby was doing, and surprisingly, about the new venture Shaun and Judith had embarked. It seemed Shaun hit his stride. The timing helped navigate a major economic downturn and having another mouth to feed.

Here's the business portion of what he wrote:

Judith suggested we find cars like I did with the Chevy to fix up and sell. We think we can do one a month until the economy comes back. Victor is still at the gas station and motivated to work nights on cars. I'm committed but afraid about such an ambitious plan.

I got busy searching for cars through the local classifieds. Victor hired two young kids to help to refurbish and sell. We got Steve who had moved to Phoenix for a job, to pipeline classic auto parts. It is like Grand Central Station—much communication needed—and I'm learning how to build a team of people who could embrace the same vision. Judith had the idea, I'm the point person, Victor is the shop, and Steve does sales and marketing.

It started taking off when Steve scaled the plan by creating a net to catch old rundown classic cars. He is developing contacts in cities where his former fraternity brothers lived. Victor is living his dream and set up a shop of his own with people willing to take a piece of the equity. Once cars are done, they sell within two weeks. The extra capital will allow me to find more mechanics and pay them by the hour. I'm kicking the plan into high gear by convincing potential partners who were mechanics or auto-body craftsmen in other cities to share my vision and expand the company.

I'll move from location to location overseeing operations and keeping classic cars coming in. Steve keeps marketing going out to target areas. Victor oversees restoration and selling. Judith stays at our "home" office keeping all the business operations moving like a skillfully constructed swiss watch. It seems like there was no end to the hours we put in but it all worked.

What was interesting, Kevin, is we had the idea around the time Judith got pregnant. Having the baby inspired our vision together.

I knew then Shaun finally crossed the precipice and was a success both personally and professionally. Over time, Shaun, Judith, and friends expanded the restoration and sales facilities into multiple cities. Four years later, I read an interview in a business publication about them working on their vision of recycling automotive transportation.

Here's an excerpt from the interview in Shaun and Judith own words:

Shaun: "I am the visionary in this operation, but visionaries have a problem when it comes to execution. And I have been blessed with a wife who can execute and deal with people, problems, and the advancement of business ideas. Her ability is the foundation of our success. I'm fortunate to have her in my life."

Judith: "You can have all of the innovation and all of the ideas, but you have to carry it through with plans to make them come to fruition. You do that by always looking at the bottom line.

Shaun: "When we met, my wife was the backbone of all operations at the radio-tower company, and her father was a lobbyist for a professional racing organization. She was no stranger to the smell of burning rubber and the sound of fuel-injected dragsters. Perhaps that's why she makes business decisions in a split second and why, when in the driver's seat, she goes from zero to sixty in no time flat."

Judith: "Shaun has a great mind for innovation. He's constantly thinking outside the box. This company wouldn't be able to function without his talent for doing that. We have great business plans and policies that have made others pay attention to what we're doing. In fact, we've knocked the socks off of many people in our business."

Interviewer: "Industry, art, nature, and history are all filled with combinations that work better together than alone. Think Proctor and Gamble, hydrogen and oxygen, Antony and Cleopatra. In creating dreams or fortunes, it's healthy to allow natural combinations to be part of the formula. You two used that formula and partnered with trusted friends to expand the entrepreneurial circle. Nicely done!"

As I look back at my friendship with Shaun, I recall the pleasure of watching a young man grow in life as well as in business. To me, his ease blending weaknesses, strengths, and dreams is evident in the relationships he enjoys today. This small company was run out of the home that Shaun and Judith first lived in after they got married. It has now become a wholesale classic car sales company that services collectors across the entire United States.

> **It has become an automobile sales company that services collectors across the entire United States.**

Outside of operational management, the company runs technical auto-shop classes to keep the pipeline full of qualified personnel and product. The regional map on the wall in the office is always highlighted with active locations. And if that's not enough, Shaun also helps oversee the locations other than the main office where Judith handles all financial, audit, tax, and payroll.

These tasks require leadership that moves through processes and directives, while acknowledging all employees' achievements. These moment-by-moment tasks also require meticulous planning, staff, resources, and contingency plans—plus an understanding that risk is always present.

A few weeks ago, I had the pleasure of Skyping with Shaun, Judith, and Bobby, who will someday be an integral part of the business. When I congratulated them on celebrating another anniversary, Judith said, "We were meant to be together, but it took time to figure out how that would work."

Then Shaun placed his head on Judith's shoulder as Bobby was making car sounds in the background. He said, "The problem is we eat, breathe, and sleep this company. But by understanding and addressing problems before they arise, we open up all options. As CEO, keeping my nose out of operations was a hard lesson for me to learn. But once we got it down, it made our lives much easier. That's when we became a successful team."

"Delegating, and letting go, is one of the secrets to your success," I said. "You two struggled to do it, but it paid for itself, again and again—especially because you surrounded yourselves with the right people. You know your own qualities and the qualities of those around you. You let others be right. Turned out to be a good choice."

Judith moved her face closer to the Skype camera and whispered loud enough for everyone to hear. "When Shaun and I got married, we weren't thinking about getting rich. Running the business was like stepping into a fire pit, and we just wanted to survive. I learned quickly that my husband wouldn't settle for mediocrity. Shaun invested his own emotional capital into all we've done—including being parents—and I feel so blessed."

With a tad of melancholy, I exercised my adopted uncle role one final time and said, "Anticipate and navigate change, and you'll never lose what you have."

> Shaun invested his own emotional capital
> into all we've done—including being parents—
> and I feel so blessed.

For Shaun and Judith, a successful marriage included a personal formula of operational execution, a first-rate partnership, and a sense of purpose that continually burned in their hearts.

You too can use Secret Success Standards from Shaun's life story like the ones below, as stepping-stones to your own accomplishments:

- Follow your overwhelming intent with a deep resolve. A rebel by nature and an iconoclast by training, Shaun saw the higher concepts of life, overcame resentment and fear, and progressed with the unlimited progression of his spirit.
- Like Shaun, know your own qualities and the qualities of those around you, then combine them to make the best choices.
- Distinguish between emotional reactions and value judgments. Look for the facts and be determined to see activities through to their natural outcomes.

CHAPTER 3

Pockets of Wealth

It never was my thinking that made the big money for me.
It always was my sitting. Got that? My sitting tight!
It is no trick at all to be right on the market.
—Edwin Lefevre

Before the COVID-19 outbreak in 2020 and the Great Recession of the late 2000s, there was a devastating stock market crash in 1929 that caused the deepest and longest economic decline in American history. The Great Depression, as it was called, lasted for almost ten years from August 1929 to June 1938. During those years, a young girl named Judy Hart learned to use setbacks as opportunities and retired in affluence.

In the summer of 1931, her world came to a screeching halt. Judy needed to drop out of high school to assist her parents in keeping the household running. Years later, she married but become a widow and was forced to raise two daughters alone. She did so with her personalized American Dream of owning a home and having financial stability to give her children a better life.

As impressive as that was, she found a way to invest in the stock market using the same techniques that made her successful as a mother and homemaker. Her investment skills made her even more remarkable. By the end of her life, she had amassed great quantities of personal, social, and financial capital in one of the hardest and scariest times in American history.

* * *

During the production of a radio segment engineered at Minnesota Public Radio, I took a needed break and was put under the charge of someone known as the station's best volunteer—Judy Hart. She had moved to Minneapolis to be close to her children and grandchildren, but she believed in keeping busy in retirement. Her smooth skin, silver hair, and blue eyes reminded me of my own grandmother we called Nana, and I was taken in by her warm, ageless personality.

The following weekend, I was happy to meet Judy again at a fundraiser for a food drive in a local park. I was invited as a guest of the station manager, and Judy and I spent the entire evening talking about her life, her philosophy, and her most important lessons on saving and investing. Reminiscences of her lessons still apply for me today and prove history is a trustworthy teacher.

Judy walked into the small but nicely appointed kitchen area that served as a green room for the radio station. I was drafting my answers to interview questions in advance of a live segment about the need for financial literacy programs. She was holding a tray with coffee, biscuits, and small packets of milk and sugar.

"The station manager thought you might need some refreshment this morning," she said as she set the tray before me. "I'm Judy Hart."

A bit startled, I said. "Hi, Judy. Nice to meet you. Is this special treatment?

"Gary sent me. He said to tell you that we treat all our guests like royalty. Would you rather have tea?" she asked.

"Coffee's fine right now, thank you. Do you work for Gary?"

"In a way."

I could tell by the twinkle of her blue eyes that she was eager to share her wisdom with me.

"A few years ago, the station participated in a community event. That's where I met Gary and asked if there were volunteer opportunities for retirees like me. He asked if I'd assist the office staff a few days a week. But I'll let you get back to your work. Let me know if you need anything else."

"Wait, don't leave yet." I said, because in an instant she had sparked the storyteller in me. "The station is fortunate to have someone like you to help. Are you from Minneapolis?"

"I was born in Chicago and lived there most of my life. I moved here seven years ago to be close to my family. I have five grandchildren!" she said with an ear-to-ear smile.

When she asked me where I was from, the usual apprehension of telling anyone west of the Mississippi the answer caught my response.

"Uh, New York, but I've lived in many different places. You have *five* grandchildren. So being a grandmother is what you do when you're not here?"

"Yes! Family is my greatest asset."

She began to turn away but nimbly stepped back and said, "Speaking of assets, I know you're here to talk about financial literacy. If you want any lessons from someone who survived the worst economic period on American history, boy, could I could tell you some tales."

Then as if embarrassed, she paused and handed me a steaming cup of coffee. "But that's not why I'm here. Enjoy your coffee!"

"Maybe I do want to hear some of your stories," I said blowing into my cup. "Do you have time to talk with me?"

"Yes, but you may not have time now. I'll be here until four this afternoon. Just ask for me after the show."

"Thanks, Judy. Count on it."

"Break a leg," she smiled closing the door.

My interview was about how to become financially free, starting early in life—from childhood through adulthood. It was also about the necessity for media to report economic information and data honestly and accurately.

Many baby boomers grew up being defined as middle class, an ideal platform that allowed people to live in comfort, choose happiness, and pursue dreams. Ongoing erosion of the middle class was causing economic polarization—or as it is said, "The rich get richer; the poor get poorer."

> ## The ongoing erosion of the middle class has caused economic polarization. The rich get richer; the poor get poorer.

As I was preparing, it occurred to me that Judy should be the one to be interviewed for the show. Afterward, I asked Gary where I could find her. He didn't know but said, "Sometimes she's in the kitchen. Sometimes she's in the conference room—the one with the bookshelves that we call our library because someone donated one of the last Encyclopedia Britannica sets ever printed, and that's where it's displayed."

I soon found Judy walking in the narrow hallway. "Do you have time to talk now?" I asked.

"Sure. Let's go into the library," she suggested, pointing in a distant direction.

"How was the show?" she asked.

"*You* should have been interviewed," I told her. "You're the one who has learned so many real-life lessons. I'm sure the things you've been through are pertinent to those who listen to the program."

"There's a lot to be said for personal experience," she replied.

> ## There's a lot to be said for personal experience.

"Living through that period in American history taught me things I didn't realize I was learning. It was tough being a child at that time but tougher to be an adult. I was lucky my parents provided a stable home life and I had siblings who made life fun. Even when we didn't have enough to eat, we still had each other. We were grateful for what we did have."

I was smitten with curiosity. "Tell me more about that time. How did you survive?"

"My dad worked with the Civilian Conservation Corps and did any side job he could get—he was strong and unafraid of hard work. In winter, he cut ice from the lake. My mom ironed clothes for people who had retained some wealth, and she did whatever else she could for what we called 'milk money.'

"Along with the neighbor kids, my brothers and I dug, planted, and maintained a vegetable garden on a plot of unused land at the end of our street, and another neighbor raised chickens. We had to be conscious—there was no other way to survive. A lot of people didn't have steady incomes at that time. That meant our clothes were hand-me-downs, always mended, and we sometimes went a long time with worn-out shoes, but we always had shelter and some food."

> **We had to be conscious—there was
> no other way to survive.**

By now, Judy was lost in her own history. The sparkle of hospitality I'd seen in her eyes when she'd brought me the coffee was gone.

"Do you know the one lesson I had no choice but to learn?" she asked. I didn't reply, but I did raise my eyebrows.

"It's patience," she said.

"These days, the world is not set up to teach patience like I learned it, and people become disappointed and distraught. There is little reward for saving and waiting for things you think you need or want. I had to wait for a lot of things early in my life.

"I didn't finish high school like my brothers did because I helped my mother with ironing. I also babysat for a neighbor who taught school—her baby was sickly. I helped with canning food. There was no room in my life for further education. My value was in assisting other people, and I worked hard after the example my parents set."

> **My value was in assisting other people, and I worked
> hard after the example my parents set.**

"Did you ever feel cheated?" It was a hard question to ask but I needed to know.

Judy didn't hesitate to answer. "No! It seemed like I was always challenged to be creative, so I could go one better than 'making do.' I missed the last two years of high school to work, but the money I made helped my family. My brothers got their high school diplomas, and when the GED first became available in 1942, my oldest brother encouraged me to take it. I took it in the summer of 1943 and passed, but it was well after I would have graduated."

Then she paused as if to look deep inside herself and added, "Maybe I did miss out, in a sort of way. Education is valuable. It should be available to all young people because it shapes them and teaches them lessons about being part of something bigger than themselves. My daughters enjoyed their years in high school, and then they worked to pay for the college classes they attended—no loans.

"Knowing what I know now, I would have studied business if I had had the opportunity to go to college. Come to think of it, very few women were in college in those days."

> **Education is valuable. It should be available to all young people because it shapes them and teaches them lessons about being part of something bigger than themselves.**

Her eyes drifted down to the floor as she continued. "When the stock market crashed in 1929, the Great Depression spread west from Wall Street like the setting sun. By the time it hit Chicago, people had already started leaving to seek new opportunities farther west."

I could see clearly in my mind's eye this young woman who probably had no idea what opportunity meant or, for that matter, what a depression was. After all, she had been living without indulgences for as long as she could remember.

At that point, as if she was reading my mind, she confirmed my thoughts.

"Yes, they were hard times, but I didn't know how hard—it seemed like others had it worse. Toward the end of that period, lots of young men left our neighborhood and never came back. I still have an old newspaper with an article that kept me praying for those boys. It was about one of our battleships being hit by German artillery. I had no idea what a 150-millimeter Howitzer was, but I knew it must be bad. Those poor men landing on that beach…it was June 6, 1944."

Then instantaneously, she paused.

Hoping to distract, I jumped in, "There's nothing good about war, but World War II did help end the Depression."

I wasn't sure if my comment would be taken the wrong way, but Judy continued unabated. "Those were the years when I kept working as a domestic, living with my parents, saving a little, and building a trousseau. I have granddaughters now who would not like knowing that my only goal was to get married and have children of my own!"

"But it sounds like you achieved your goal. I can only imagine how hard it must have been in those days," I uttered reassuringly.

"I did achieve my goal. And when I was twenty-five, I married the love of my life, Leon Hart."

"What made him the love of your life?" I asked, seeing the lovelight in her eyes.

"He was kind to me whenever I went to buy at the butcher shop his father owned. He treated me with dignity but was firm when it was in our best interest. And oh my, did we laugh! Sometimes I laughed until I cried. We grew to respect each other, and our love flourished.

"Before we married, Leon inherited the business and it kept him out of the war—but he wished he had gone. Personally, I was happy not to be one of those military brides, but we never talked about it much because I knew he had mixed emotions. Like most men of that day, he wanted to show love of country," she said.

> **Like most men of that day, he wanted to show love of country.**

"Occasionally, he'd walk to the west side by the Chicago River between West Adams and West Jackson. He'd walk for nine and a half city blocks with his dog, so he could be where the trains pulled away from Union Station taking hundreds of men to war. It was as if he needed to be on one of those trains."

There was love in her eyes but soon a cloud of compassion blocked their brilliance as she recounted the realities of a country at war.

"It was toward the end of World War II, we got married on August 17th, 1945, a beautiful summer day. The country was at its wits end with the fighting and loss of life. There was rationing. Everybody had a book containing removable stamps for items that were in demand: sugar, meat, cooking oil. You couldn't get those things without a stamp.

"Because of the pressure the country was under, we spent our honeymoon in Indiana. That weekend, Leon told me he was tired of being a butcher. The work was hard, the money wasn't good, and he wanted to try something different on his own."

Judy's lips sealed as her neck stretched in a look to heaven. "He was a sensitive man, and during those hard times when people were poor, he gave away as much as he sold. When we returned to our apartment over the shop that Monday after our honeymoon weekend, we closed the business, and Leon got a job with the telephone company. It made our lives better because he was happier. He no longer smelled like beef and didn't have to work through dinner managing orders for other people's meals."

The glimmer in Judy's crystal-blue eyes began to radiate again. "They were good times and I miss them. Leon had a dog named Tramper. He saved the pup from being euthanized, and Tramper never left his side—so many warm memories with a man and man's best friend."

Judy looked up, fearful she had gone on too long, but she could see my full attention and continued.

"Time did fly by. I worked doing ironing for extra money until my girls arrived one after another—Helen in October 1946 and Rosemary in January 1949. Out of room, we moved to a little cottage on a tree-lined street with a picket fence. Compared to what it had been like in the Depression, life got better and better for me. Plus, I loved being a mother."

> **Compared to what it had been in the Depression, life got better and better. I loved being a mother.**

The room we were conversing in was overcrowded with classic books and heavy-duty storage file boxes. Yet by now I felt like I was in the living room of her old home.

"So you stayed home with your girls when they were young?" I asked.

"Yes. To me, family means more than anything. I took on a lot of responsibility for rearing the girls and keeping our household running. But I also wanted to keep working along with Leon and found a way to work *and* maintain a home once the girls went to school."

That piqued my curiosity. I leaned forward to hear more.

Judy elaborated, "I was used to making and managing money—I'd developed a consciousness about money at a young age. I wanted my girls to have that same understanding too, even though their lives were much easier than mine. Leon and I provided for them, but I paid them allowance money and expected them to do chores. I encouraged them to get jobs babysitting when they were young."

> **I'd developed a consciousness about money
> at a young age.**

Recalling my childhood coziness as my own nana read in her warm and comforting voice, I settled deeper into my chair. I hoped she could not detect the faint lackadaisical smile on my lips.

"Like my mom, I took in ironing for 'milk money'—only I didn't use it for milk. Leon came home from work one day in the early 1950s with an information packet about a pension plan, and we read every page about how it worked. It included telephone company stock and stock from other publicly traded companies."

She took another breath. "I had some fear about stocks crashing. Leon had none and I did, but I decided to follow his example. We signed up to participate in both Part A, the employer contribution lifetime benefit, and in Part B based on our added contributions, but we started with small amounts."

Judy got up and walked over to gaze out the window. The sun, sinking under a bank of clouds, illuminated the room with a church like radiance. She lowered the blinds and turned on a lamp. "The light went on in my head—just like this!" Judy remembered.

"You mean about the pension?"

"Yes. Leon and I talked for hours about how our money could make its own money. We kept some savings for my peace of mind—to cover household emergencies—but we wanted the girls to be able to go to college, we wanted to pay off our mortgage, and we wanted to be able to stop working someday. I started to pay closer attention to the things I bought such as groceries, clothes, and home goods. When I saw how money from my purchases went into companies' profits and their profits could come back to me through dividends, I wanted to be part of that process!"

> When I saw how money from my purchases went into companies' profits and their profits could come back to me through dividends, I wanted to be part of that process!

"You were wife, mother, and investor. How did you keep track of it all.?" I asked.

She paused long enough for me to think we were done for the day and then pondered, "No one's ever asked me that question before. But having a focus on my worth helped me, I think.

"You see, I was attuned to the business of running a home and family—even with the side jobs I did when the girls were very young. Leon's salary kept a roof over our heads and food on the table. I needed to do my part. We shared the same goals in wanting a happy family life for ourselves, raising responsible children, and being good citizens. But what kept us talking to one another all the time was my interest in investing."

I was captivated. Most couples are overwhelmed by all the layers of domestic life—the routines, the schedules of family members, maintenance of a home, yard, pets, automobiles, school, and all the extracurricular activities. Some couples divide and conquer to keep up with the logistics. Judy and Leon seemed to have hit on a formula that also included net-worth advancement, and I wanted to know more.

> Judy and Leon seemed to have hit on a formula for happiness in net-worth advancement.

"This sounds rather unusual. You two worked hand-in-hand focusing on having a healthy family life and a healthy financial life and grew your assets. Is that correct?"

Judy was pleased I recognized how unique this was and willfully replied, "Yes, Leon watched the stocks in our pension plan until he could use a small portion of our savings to make our first independent investment. In those days, we walked a few blocks to Northern Trust in Chicago where we could place a stock order. We bought a few shares of General Electric and celebrated when we got our first small dividend check. A little later, we budgeted to spend forty-five dollars a month on stocks."

My first thought was how small of an amount that was, but in the context of the time, I quickly became impressed. "You were saving money. You were investing. You were paying attention. All great strategies for getting ahead financially to live a good life."

"A good life," Judy exclaimed. "What is a good life? You were probably a little kid when people started buying on credit and carrying credit card balances. The idea of 'get it now, pay later' never made sense to Leon or me. We had our household income and expense budget. When we wanted to buy an expensive item like new furniture, a new car, or a color TV, we planned for it. We saved and waited until we could pay cash.

"Sure, we had credit cards, but we paid off the balance each month, except for a few times when we had other unexpected expenses. One year, Leon needed surgery, and it was the same year we had to replace a car that turned out to be a lemon.

"But let me tell you about a good life. It's not about money. It's about taking care of yourself and your family. Get those two things operating well and then you can expand anywhere."

Judy had an adamant tone in her voice that I had not heard yet as she continued.

"I'm a big believer in adding good things back to the community, too. I helped at the school when my daughters were there, and we participated in community-outreach with our church."

> I'm a big believer in adding good things back to the community, too.

I could see her moral fiber was as deep as the thick impenetrable ice her father once cut with a chain saw from the frozen lake to pay for food during the Depression.

"Good point," I said, not letting on what I was thinking. "You have your priorities straight. Doing things right and not procrastinating is planting seeds of hope that pay enormous dividends."

Again, Judy was lost in her history and took a moment to respond.

"And I appreciate everything I have," she said with the enthusiasm of a sixteen-year-old on prom night.

The hustle and bustle around the station was fading out like the end of a record. The only sound came from studio monitors down the hall that had replaced the chatter of business.

"Looking back on my life, I see that living through the Depression taught me to value things highly. For example, if you have to wait for something, then finally getting it becomes a more meaningful experience." Apparently, Judy had no intent of leaving the station on time, so I nestled in for more simple wisdoms.

"We didn't need an overpriced financial plan," she scolded. "To me, cooking an apple pie for a sick neighbor or watching a friend's dog, or giving a simple smile that showed concern was my mission. Those efforts returned enough goodwill to keep me solvent."

Then a sigh swept away her laughter. "My childhood was a training ground for all I have today. Yes, we faced many adversities while living through that economic crisis, but we always remained compassionate. I have memories of hard times but no bitterness— we took care of each other," she summarized.

> **I have memories of hard times but no bitterness.**

Then with a burst of laughter, she said, "And I kept money in the cookie jar!"

"The cookie jar?" I said in a low barely audible voice. "Did I hear you correctly?"

"Yes, every week, I would set aside cash from my home-based jobs in the cookie jar on our kitchen counter. When the amount reached a few hundred dollars, I'd remove the bills and put them in order by denomination. Then I'd fold the bills and place the roll into the pocket of my apron and set my mind on buying stock that paid good dividends. Once I had some ideas, I'd wait for Leon to come home so we could talk about it after dinner."

Seeing her newly acquired animated style, I laughed out loud. "Your cookie jar money has given a whole new meaning to the term!"

"We also reinvested our dividends," she lashed back.

"I loved doing the research—which was nothing more than talking to my friends about the products they liked and going to the library to read about the sales statistics of certain products. I was always looking for possibilities. It was like going on an in-the-kitchen shopping spree. As I worked in my kitchen, going from appliance to appliance, I'd fiddle with the bills in my pocket and wonder what the company made or how it was related to each. I'd get excited to tell Leon what moved me that day. Once, we bought stock in a company that made instant-picture cameras. That was high tech at the time!"

> **I was always looking for possibilities. It was like going on an in-the-kitchen shopping spree.**

I could tell Judy embraced life all around her. The black and white images from Polaroid cameras were the rage of her generation and were as innovative and popular in the 1950s as Instagram is now. Like social media icons of today, Edwin Land left Harvard and used science to invent a product people could enjoy in everyday life.

Judy was "cool" in her day and put big-hearted faith in ordinary things. She understood little about theoretical debates on the economy but rejoiced to find herself among modern technological marvels in the kitchen. To her at that time, they represented a creative manufacturing revolution that was making America great—and she was right.

It was Friday and, unlike earlier in the workday, a stillness had fallen on the radio station. The peacefulness remined me of my radio days working the graveyard shift during grad school. I didn't want the time to end, but I instinctively glanced at my watch.

Judy interrupted my thoughts. "Speaking of possibilities, look at the time! It's nearly five-thirty."

"Wow, I'm sure you have to be somewhere," I said. "We've talked for a long time."

"Oh my! I am going to meet one of my daughters at soccer. Then we're going to take the kids out for pizza. It was nice talking with you."

"You've done amazing things in your life. I wish we had more time," I said.

"Maybe no better and no worse than anyone else," she replied as she collected her coat, hat, purse, and scarf. "I hope to see you again someday."

I stayed behind in the makeshift room defined by the encyclopedias. It had become an inner sanctum for me, and I was tempted to run my fingers through the knowledge in those old loosely bound books. As I turned the brittle pages and smelled the old dust, I kept thinking about Judy. For someone without an advanced education, she bravely relied on practical information to start her research. Leon had been so impressed with her stock-picking advice; he frequently discussed his wife's insights with men at work when they shared advice with each other about investing in their pension plans. *What an exciting time the 1950s must have been*, I thought.

> **For someone without an advanced education, Judy bravely relied on empirical information to start her research.**

Flipping through the delicate pages, I was careful but hoped a tactile knowledge would pulse through me. I stopped at the Great Depression. It took until 1954 for the Dow Jones Industrial Average to finally surpass its pre-crash peak in 1929. *A twenty-five-year recovery*, I thought. Completely unaware of this global trend, Judy had invested only in products she loved and also reinvested the dividends month after month.

Scared by the crash and the Great Depression that followed, most people in her generation stayed away from buying stocks. In 1952, only 4.2 percent of the U.S. population was investing in the stock market. Judy and Leon clearly were well ahead of this trend and were working hard to find their American Dream. *What a time it must have been*, I mused.

That weekend, Gary invited me to a fundraising event in the local park. I went as a guest of the radio station and was surprised to find Judy with someone who looked like a younger version of her seated at a picnic table, along with two even younger versions of both grandma and daughter.

"Hi, Judy. I was thinking about all the remarkable things you shared with me Friday. I realized you would have been considered a bottom-up investor in your day. Clearly ahead of your time," I said, complementing her.

"Nice to see you again, Kevin. This is my daughter, Helen."

I noticed Helen had Judy's smile, thick blonde hair, and the same sparkle in her blue eyes. "Nice to meet you, Helen. Your mother is a remarkable woman," I said.

Judy turned to her daughter. "Helen, this is the man who listened to my life story. I think it's his turn to tell us all about him!"

"Just how much did Mom tell you?" Helen asked. But before I could answer, she turned to her mother and said, "I'll bet you didn't tell him about Dad."

> ### I'll bet you didn't tell him about Dad.

Judy's face went blank.

In defense I uttered, "When we said good-bye, you and Leon were living the American Dream." I smiled clumsily.

Helen, less jovial, returned, "When I was ten, my dad died. It was sudden. Unexpected," she said with a touch of anger in her voice. "An aneurysm. I was devastated—he was my hero. I know it was hard for Mom, too, but my younger sister and I never heard how she dealt with the sorrow."

Judy's mood turned somber. "No, Helen. Why would I go into details with a child? You know I don't dwell on negative things."

"I realize how much strength my mom had, and now having my own kids, I appreciate her so much. Not many women could've done what she did," Helen added.

"Maybe we were living the dream," Judy said as she turned back to face me, "but it wasn't intentional. I just learned to adapt at an early age. I'd adjust any situation to make it a benefit. And that's exactly what I did after Leon died."

She continued, "His death was more difficult than living through the Great Depression. Leon was a deep and only true love of mine. But I had the girls. I had to keep going. Do you know the meaning of SAR? It's an abbreviation for the equation 'situation plus adjustment equals reward.'"

Brilliant! I thought. Such natural wisdom.

To see Judy smile that day, one would never have believed she'd ever had a minute of sadness in her life. Her world was about people and possibilities. She never met pain with resentment or anger but with insight and compassion.

> **Judy never met pain with resentment or anger but with insight and compassion.**

"I did feel sorrow," Judy said. "Occasionally we'd take a ride back to where I'd first met Leon. His butcher shop had been turned into a candy store. It was as if God put it there for me to sit with the girls and remember my happy times.

"We'd linger at the counter sipping black-and-white ice cream sodas, and the smell of the soda fountain would take me through memories of growing up. Healing started happening all around me. I let trust guide my life while accepting Leon's loss without bitterness. He had worked so hard at his job on the phone lines, and because he cared so much about us, I focused on gratitude."

In her young life, Judy had dealt with things according to how she felt they fit into her personal value system. Sadness about Leon's death was no exception, although it likely lingered for years. Being the mother of two daughters forced her to quickly regroup.

Using her gracious, creative, and richly developed insights, Judy took complete responsibility for her family, her actions, and the actions of her children.

"I did my part," Judy resumed. "I worked, saved, and scarified my whole life. Leon always insisted we put away a small portion of what we made, which wasn't that much."

The corners of her mouth turned up. "I'd say, 'You are such a squirrel,' and he'd look at me and reply, 'Judy, someday you're going to be glad I'm a squirrel.' Well, I *was* glad! In those years together, we'd squirreled away enough money to bridge the gap between being trapped and being able to hold out for something better," Judy said.

> We'd squirreled away enough money to bridge the gap between being trapped and being able to hold out for something better.

As we sat beneath the tall trees, the air grew cooler. Bodies all around us were in motion for a good cause and again, time quickly passed with Judy.

"Leon died too soon, she continued but I remembered all the fun we'd had, like when we walked to the stock company at the corner to watch the board. I learned plenty!" She wiped a tear.

"I'm never bitter. I'm grateful for the time we had together.," she added. "These days, I'm amazed how people take equity loans on their homes to buy things like vacations and clothes. People would rather look at what someone else can do for them than work toward a goal. Leon and I never used loans or margin accounts or fancy annuities—or let salespeople persuade us to buy something. That's just how we were.

"I count myself as one of the most blessed people around. Living through the Great Depression and doing without a lot of luxuries was difficult, but it made me appreciate the value of honest work and especially the reward that comes from helping others less fortunate find their way. I believe in giving a helping hand—not a handout," she said proudly.

> **I believe in giving a helping hand—not a handout.**

"When Leon died, he left me with his pension, some money from social security, a mortgage I paid down with his life insurance money, and stocks in our portfolio. These days, I'm able to volunteer at the radio station and other places in this community.

"And now, it's time for you to tell me your story, Kevin. How have you learned to invest your time, talents, and money to guarantee rewards for your future?"

"I'm working on it," I replied with a grin. "It's interesting to me, Judy, that we're here to support a food bank that assists people who are victims of yet another economic downturn. In your life, you came close to relying on a charity such as this, but your creativity and integrity of spirit led you to create a community garden and work in order to save. Then later, you learned to save and invest."

"It's the American Dream to be happy in your own way," she said, responding to my comment. "And happiness is possible, no matter how much money you have in the bank. The fun is in making a plan and living by it as if it were a map leading to abundance—both material and spiritual."

As evening approached, Judy, Helen, and I enjoyed several topics of conversation and savory Midwest home-cooked food. When it was time to go, we exchanged contact information. We stayed in touch over the next three years, and in the spring of 2005, I got a call from Helen with sad news.

Judy had passed away that winter, and she thought her mom might want me to know the rest of her story.

"Thank you, Helen, and please accept my sympathy," I said after composing myself. "I would have sent flowers had I known, but I will send a memorial contribution if a fund had been established."

"Thanks, that is kind of you," Helen said, "but Judy set up her own fund that's kind of unusual."

"What is it?" I asked.

"Well one day, my mom received a call from the branch manager where she bought her stocks. He told her the company would have to close her account if she didn't come in to update her investor profile information.

"Mom was really aging by then and asked us to accompany her to see him. Sitting in his large mahogany office with its big window looking out on the trading floor made me feel like we were in a fishbowl. I wondered why all these people were looking in at us."

As Helen spoke, I adjusted my cell phone for a better signal.

"As it turned out, Mom was kind of famous for meticulously making regular deposits to her account, owning odd lots of stocks, and reinvesting the dividends with available cash. By so doing, she'd turned it into a two-and-a-half-million-dollar account.

"We were shocked! Rosemary and I just sat there looking at each other. I will never forget the look on Mom's face. The branch manager asked if something was wrong, and Mom just said, 'No. I was just startled because I thought I heard my late husband laughing.'"

Helen and I talked for almost an hour that night about reminiscences of Judy. I was happy to learn that, in her final days, she had remained compassionate and involved.

During the month of Judy's final Christmas, she took the long train ride to the old neighborhood. After seeing her longtime friend and physician, she walked down the street, peered in the window of the old candy store, and continued to the animal shelter where Leon once rescued his dog. There, she wrote a check for five thousand dollars, saying, "I promised to never have another dog, but I want one now."

> **There, she wrote a check for five thousand dollars, saying, "I promised to never have another dog, but I want one now."**

The shelter manager was happy to accept the contribution and obligingly gave her an abandoned puppy. On the spot, she named it Tramper.

At home, Judy tried to forget what she had been told at the doctor's office and prepared for a wonderful Christmas with her family. On New Year's Day, when the girls called, she insisted on being alone, and they respected her wishes.

Close to the end of the phone call, Helen was unable to hold back tears. She told me that, on January 2nd, she and Rosemary found their mother lifeless. She was sitting upright in her rocking chair with Tramper stretched out protectively across her feet.

Judy's last will and testament made financial allowances for her two children and five grandchildren. It also bequeathed $250,000 to a handful of local charities in the small suburban town where they all lived. Tramper was willed to Rosemary, who lived only a few blocks away.

"And thanks to my mom," Helen said with resolve in her voice, "in every Independence Day parade, Tramper rides shotgun on the fire truck. It's paid for in full from a donation from that sentimental woman—my mom—who simply wanted safety and security for us and the community where we lived."

To end my phone call with Helen, I could only say, "Thank you. Your words touched me deeply—as did your mother. I will always remember what she taught me about the living of financial literacy and how to meet any economic storm clouds in any generation."

You too can use Secret Success Standards from Judy's life story like the ones below, as stepping-stones to your own accomplishments:

- Invest materially and emotionally into all aspects of what you love. Hold lots of memories but no bitterness. Replace any resentment or anger with insight and compassion.
- Align your investments with your genuine interests in humankind and your intuitive awareness. Invest a small portion of what you make and reinvest your dividends to make money on your money.
- Have the discipline to wait for what you want. Evaluate the changing landscape before taking the next step. Be willing to say no to anything less than what you desire.

CHAPTER 4

Wings of a Plan

My wish is to stay always like this,
living quietly in a corner of nature.
—**Claude Monet**

During a summer on Long Island, I received a call from my friend Peter Churchfield. He asked me to join his wildlife rescue team in a vast natural recreation area that includes the states of New Jersey, Pennsylvania, and a large ridge of the Appalachian Mountains. Our mission was to determine the security of a nesting area for two bald eagle fledglings that were capable of flight but possibly still nest-dependent and vulnerable.

When a possible poaching incident was reported, Peter's team was mobilized to hike in, observe, photograph, and record activity around the nesting area over a three-day period and report back to the Park Service.

I had known Peter over the span of his career in sales. We'd met in an elevator at my office building when I overheard him talking about being a wildlife rescue volunteer. Intrigued, I got out on the same floor as he did and asked for more information. He was willing to oblige—and our friendship and my volunteerism began.

I knew that Peter had strong beliefs and sometimes struggled with inflexibility, but he never ran away from a problem. Instead, he forged bad breaks into opportunities by finding ways to improve his life. Somehow, though, he always seemed to be last in line when it came to getting a good break—unless it was a broken bone from a sporting accident. Nonetheless, he made the hard decisions and accepted ownership of all consequences.

Peter and I had not seen each other in years. After we completed our work with eagles in the Delaware Water Gap, we went camping as a reward. What happened that evening in the wild taught me as much about nature as it did about Peter—who had made a fortune while those around him were losing theirs.

* * *

Peter grew up in Cleveland near the shore of Lake Erie, which is the tenth or twelfth largest lake in the world, depending on which local you ask. The lake is largely responsible for Cleveland's unpredictable and often severe weather. Lake oscillations called Seiches can randomly whip up winds that last indefinitely. In winter, subfreezing temperatures can snap in without warning and continue for weeks.

On one such subfreezing Tuesday, Peter Churchfield and his wife, Wendy, packed up their car and their two young children and left Cleveland forever. They headed south for New Jersey and a fresh start in life.

Peter's love of nature influenced his life and forged our relationship. He was inspired by water, was conscious of Lake Erie's pollution problems, and was troubled because he felt powerless to solve them. After Ohio's Cuyahoga River caught fire one summer, he became committed to keeping a small part of the world pristine.

> **Peter remained committed to keeping a small part of the world pristine.**

When Peter wasn't involved in eco-volunteerism or selling office machines to companies ranging from mom-and-pops to Fortune 100s, he liked to relax while fishing in a clear, cold mountain stream. He loved to feel the tackle bending in his hand and the tug of a feisty trout grabbing a fly in his game of catch and release.

Now that he had been retired for a few years, his passion for fishing and clean water had intensified. We shared that love of the outdoors and both spent time helping to keep it in good condition from opposite sides of the country. We also shared by phone our experiences of enjoying the peace of campfires, sleeping among the trees, and eating breakfast to the sound of rushing water. Finally, we had the opportunity to do it together.

Over the years, Peter's life had been a lot of give and take. At one point, he even suffered a broken neck. Yet with stamina and resolve, he found his way from a minimum-wage job on a factory floor to a sales job where he would excel.

But during that weekend we spent in the wilderness, it was a complete stranger who mysteriously revealed a new truth about how Peter accumulated his wealth.

Millions of years of seismic uplift and glacial activity had formed an S-shaped pass through mountains called the Delaware Water Gap. It was here where Peter had found a place to retreat and enjoy his leisure time.

Nestled within a familiar ravine, Peter and I set up a camp surrounded by past-blooming hemlocks and rhododendrons in late July. Peter's deluxe trailer equipped with top-notch gear was quite a contrast to the simple camp where we'd just spent the previous three nights. In fewer than twelve miles, we had gone from a one-star to a five-star accommodation, and I was more than ready.

I was feeling the aftermath of search-and-rescue fatigue. After three days of monitoring bald eagles with a rough-and-tumble group and sleeping on the ground, I looked forward to a comfy rest. While Peter gathered tinder to build the evening's campfire, I sat against a rock, using my rolled-up sleeping bag as a cushion.

"You have the energy I wish I had. Thanks for setting up camp," I said. "No problem, buddy. When I bring Wendy and Kimberly up here, they sit around and watch me work, too!" Peter said with a familiar cynicism laced with warmth.

Peaking at the time on my cell phone, I selfishly thought, "Perfect time to rest awhile."

While Peter worked, we talked about the place we had come to love over the years. The Gap, as he called it, reminded him of his childhood on the shore of Lake Erie. In both places, he could take a deep breath, focus, and consider things according to how *he* felt, not how *society* thought he should feel.

Thinking of my own childhood, I said, "We both were fortunate to grow up near natural places where we could escape. For me, it was the surrounding bays, inlets, and miles of waves as far as you can see breaking on soft white sand."

Stifling a yawn with my hand, I said, "Miss it terribly sometimes."

"Life's about to get better, pal! Here, help me with this hammock. You can stretch out, read a book, and get some rest."

After we connected the hammock between two trees, Peter gave me a pillow from the camper. I climbed in and tuned in to the sounds of nature: flowing water, birdsong, rustling leaves. The hammock's gentle sway felt hypnotic.

Next thing I remembered was the sun setting well behind the trees and hearing Peter talking with someone. I opened my eyes to see a short, pear-shaped man with thinning hair. He seemed to be in his early sixties.

"Meet Bernie," Peter said as I cleared the sleep from my eyes. "When I saw you fall asleep, I hiked downstream thinking I was completely alone, and in the middle of nowhere, Bernie's camp just appeared. We're neighbors so I asked him to join us for dinner. You hungry yet?"

"Always, but I'll help."

"Bernie has fish to share," Peter said.

Bernie raised a handful of freshly caught trout high in the air, then turned to Peter. "Nice camp you have here. Impressive."

Peter, tan with graying hair, still possessed his athleticism and was the image of gallantry. "Thanks, Bernie. You know, I've been coming here for over thirty years and never met another person."

"Maybe that's because you're set up like the Ritz Carlton. That's the best outfitted travel trailer I've ever seen. It looks like a hotel on wheels. Other campers sense the high real estate and stay away!"

"That's not my intent," Peter laughed. "I do value privacy, but this state-of-the-art setup makes it so I can have the best of both worlds."

"I'm just messing with you," Bernie smiled. "I sold off all my camping gear—minimized to a one-person tent, sleeping bag, tackle box, canteen, and cooler—and not by choice.

"I'll be back with some garnishes."

As Bernie walked toward the river, I turned to Peter. "This is going to be interesting. What a surprise. I never suspected that we'd have a guest at our campfire tonight."

"Well, Wendy has always said that you don't know a stranger until you speak to him," he replied.

"True. The day I shared an elevator with you, it was the same thing."

"Glad you did. We've had some great adventures together, Kevin," he said while laying out the pan, utensils, and plates. "Trout's our main course, and we have whole-wheat crackers, apples, and a jar of olives to share with the new guy. If all goes well, we'll bring out the brandy later."

Out of the woods Bernie appeared again, this time with a large can of beans. He placed it next to Peter who was cooking the fish in olive oil, sea salt, and cracked pepper.

Our dinner conversation centered on the food, the eagle rescue project, Bernie's big fish catches, and restoring nature.

"Nature is one thing," Bernie interrupted, "but restoring the economy is another. In addition to nice camping gear, I had a lot of other nice things: cars, boats, and even an equity share in a plane. When the crash happened, it all went to the bank. I almost lost my house."

I didn't know how to respond. It seemed that Bernie was jealous of Peter, and I wondered how much Peter had told this man about himself. After dinner as we collected our empty plates, Peter excused himself without explanation.

Left awkwardly alone with Bernie, I said, "Once I started learning how long and how much it takes to save enough money to buy things, I realized I really didn't need them!"

> **Once I started learning how long and how much it takes to save enough money to buy things, I realized I really didn't need them!**

"I wish I could say that," he replied. "There was a time when if I *could* buy it, I *did* buy it. And I had it all. I had a college education, a young wife, a nice house. I just kept adding until forces other than the ones I had control over started subtracting."

I wondered how to diplomatically ask for details, but my head was feeling weary, and I wanted to climb back into the hammock.

Mustering some energy, I asked, "Did you say you worked in engineering?"

"Yes, I worked at several companies over the years. My divorce was final three months before I got laid off, and the market swept away much of what was left. As good as I was at design, I was not good at designing my own house of cards."

I felt even more uncomfortable now and all I could say was, "I'm sorry." Then I went about the chore of cleaning up after dinner.

"I get it," Peter said with eyes of a Cheshire Cat coming out of the darkness. "I was listening—don't forget to put the trash in the trunk so the critters can't get at it, Kevin. Here are the keys."

Peter then walked the short distance to the fire pit and said, "Bernie, I moved to New Jersey to start a new life working in sales. The factory job I left in Ohio had no promise, and I made a vow to do whatever it took to create success."

Bending closer to Bernie, Peter sympathized, "Then that crash in 2008—the one that will go down in the history books—happened. A lot of my friends had the same experience as you. A job in sales is different from engineering; you probably had a salary. I had only a small salary, so the commission was everything to me. My energy was tied to constant performance and an obsession with the flow of cash."

Bernie shook his head as if it had come loose. "I thought pulling in my six-figure salary would be all glory. Little did I know I'd be broke by 2009."

"A lot of people went broke," Peter consoled. "Average people who worked hard, saved, and invested in their own homes went broke. When I think about how this downfall was based on the way property debt was gambled with, it totally disgusts me."

"So how did you dodge the bullet, Peter?"

Having overheard Bernie's million-dollar question, I slammed the trunk on the trash bags and walked close enough to listen but far enough away not to participate.

The two men had totally different life situations, yet under the power of this cathedral of nature, they were openly exposing their deepest secrets. I learned that Pete's life was not without crisis.

When Lehman Brothers, a Wall Street firm where my sister-in-law worked, filed for bankruptcy, Peter was not knee-deep in debt. Rather, he was knee-deep in a cold running stream holding his fishing rod. But the day Merrill Lynch needed to be acquired by Bank of America to avoid the same, Peter was distressed. He gave me a call, one that I vividly remembered almost a decade earlier.

That was the day I summarized that the problems were due primarily to exposure of packaged subprime loans and credit-default swaps. Peter understood the aggregate of events but intuitively knew things were about to get worse.

The dominoes did fall one by one, and the crisis rapidly reached global proportions resulting in bank failures in Europe and sharp reductions in equity prices worldwide. In Iceland, devaluation of its currency, the Króna, almost caused a government bankruptcy. In America, when the U.S. government seized control of AIG, one of the world's biggest insurance companies, it sent out shock waves. The net asset value of a primary money-market fund fell below one dollar, "breaking the buck." Depositors began withdrawing funds.

> Peter understood the aggregate of events but
> intuitively knew things were about to get worse.

Over those weeks, I spent many hours on the phone giving Peter updates—but there was one thing I couldn't share. It was private information about a handful of Congressional leaders who, as lifetime politicians with limited practical business experience, panicked and wanted to invoke martial law. They called for a secret meeting with Treasury Secretary Henry Paulson and Federal Reserve Chairman Bernanke in Nancy Pelosi's office.

Fortunately, Bernanke, a former professor of economics at Princeton, and Paulson, who had run the large investment firm of Goldman Sachs, prevailed with level heads. Instead of chaos, a practical course of action was put in place.

But for those deepest in debt, the plan couldn't put the economic carnage genie back in the bottle. Over the next eight years, tens of thousands of Americans slipped into the financial abyss—Bernie being one of them. A cold sweat of remembrances came over me. I tuned back to hear their conversation.

"So, Peter, did you get hurt in the crash?" Bernie brazenly asked without a touch of diplomacy.

I watched Peter pace on soft pine needles, his eyes fixated on the ground. The long shadow cast by the campfire made him look gigantic. Then he stopped and turned. "Did I get hurt? Beyond a shadow of a doubt! My house value and my portfolio went down like a rock. *Everything* went down. I had friends who went completely broke. But was I in deep trouble?" That's when Peter flashed a TV-ready smile. "Not really. Because my situation was simple."

Bernie was stunned. "How does one succeed even in the hardest of all times?"

"I owned everything outright," Peter said. "And if my house was suddenly worth half of what I paid for it, so be it. I didn't owe anybody *anything*. Yeah, I was outraged about what had happened. But personally, I was okay."

> I was outraged about what had happened to the global financial markets. But personally, I was okay.

Turning his head like an owl stalking prey, Peter peered at me, standing in the darkness. "Hey, what are you thinking about over there, Palmer?"

Startled, I needed to come up with something plausible. "Uh, thinking about all those conversations we had during that time. Three months after Lehman fell, President George W. Bush signed the Emergency Economic Stabilization Act, creating the TARP Program, to purchase failing bank assets. Remember that, Peter?"

He knew I was dancing, but I continued without a breath. "Bailing people out after they made their own careless, greedy mistakes wasn't how we were raised!"

"That's for sure," Peter shot back. "I grew up with blue-collar parents in a working-class neighborhood. I was guided by values that provided a litmus test for right and wrong. I learned from my mistakes without blaming others. There was a kind of 'your conscience will guide you' philosophy that cut to the chase of issues. I learned to listen to my soul and then move on to accomplish things without wasting time.

"I was impulsive as a kid—spoke without thinking first but learned how to keep calm, drop the drama, and talk problems through. My strong family unit supported me and taught me a work ethic that I used to every advantage," Peter proudly added, letting me off the hook.

I walked over to the cooler, grabbed three beers, twisted off the tops, and put one in each of their outstretched hands. Then I pulled over a log to lean on.

> **My strong family unit supported me and taught me a work ethic that I used to every advantage.**

"By age twelve," Peter told Bernie, "I learned that buying my own clothes gave me freedom. I saved up and used my allowance for a Milwaukee Brewers cap."

Bernie took a long sip of his cold beer. "I guess a supportive family makes a difference, but how did that work for you?"

"Perhaps it started when I took responsibility for my dad's car," Peter said. "He let me use it on the weekends. After I brought it home, I washed it and cleaned the garage to make sure I'd be allowed to borrow it again."

"Guess you had to start somewhere," Bernie said, feeling cheated by the answer.

"Oh, there's more to him than that," I injected. "Tell him about your college days, Peter."

"Well, I got into school on an athletic scholarship, but it ended when I broke my neck pole vaulting." He gave Bernie a matter-of-fact look and flashed that Peter smile of acceptance. "At that time, it was just the way it was. I could no longer compete, so my scholarship was taken away. No lawyers, no lawsuits; I just lost my funding."

"That would be an outrage by today's college standards," Bernie exclaimed.

"You're right," Peter reinforced. "Today, students wouldn't lose their scholarships, they'd go to an attorney! I just went on and found a way to stay in school."

I was proud of Peter's story and chimed in on behalf of my friend. "Peter's moral code is that challenges were meant to be overcome without blame or excuses. Why would he stop his life over a mere broken neck and lost money?" I asked with my usual tongue-and-cheek sarcasm.

"After spending seven weeks in the hospital, he gathered himself, neck brace and all, and transferred to a different college. He paid for it on his own, but it proved to be more than he could manage. Strapped with bills and wanting desperately to stay in school, he did the unthinkable; he began practicing so he could compete for another athletic scholarship. In what today would probably cause a public-relations firestorm, he earned a second athletic scholarship."

Bernie gave Peter a look of disbelief.

"I have a tendency to hit walls," Peter added. "In what would seem like enough physical pain for any one person, I sustained subsequent injuries in my life that required seventeen orthopedic operations."

Bernie sucked air through his teeth. "Holy Moses!"

"I got through them all and feel very blessed today," Peter responded.

The darkness of night now totally engulfed the clearing where we three stood around the fire. Beyond the trees, we could see nothing.

"Peter, you worked hard and worked a lot," I said proudly. "You got it all without luck, a lottery ticket, or a reality show contract. You didn't expect something for nothing."

Bernie brushed back his thinning hair with a flat hand. "That wasn't how most of my friends made their money. I hung around people who got rich speciously. That's why listening to you talk makes me uncomfortable. You took the high road; they took any road.

"The way I grew up," Bernie continued, "if you were at the best schools or highest levels of business, there were always ways to cheat the system. I watched it happen. It's worse in the public sector. Cheating the system is rampant. Those kinds of people don't add to creating jobs whatsoever."

In that moment, I saw the need for everyone to take a breath. I said, "Bernie, Peter's strong financial sense came over time selling office copiers and printers, not from reading theory in college textbooks. But it's his ability to quickly recover from adversity that kept him on track. He believes it was his old-fashioned courage and unwavering honesty that supported his quiet success."

> Peter's old-fashioned courage and unwavering honesty supported his quiet success.

With everyone relaxing again, I continued telling Peter's story. "In college, to supplement his meager scholarship, he took classes at night and found employment with a company that made diesel engines. After he graduated, Peter could have worked in an office, but he chose the factory floor so he could work as many hours as possible."

"Thanks, buddy. You know my story well," Peter added. "I worked six or seven days a week and had to buy steel-toed shoes that I always took off before I entered my home to see my new wife. I didn't want to track in oil and metal clippings.

"During one stretch, I worked for forty-two days without time off during an assembly line shutdown. That's when I had a chance to rise. I had to collaborate with others and earn their respect, so I came up with a solution that even the bosses had missed. That was my greatest lesson in diplomacy."

Peter continued, "I could have used the situation to my advantage and moved up the ranks, but I was tired of Ohio, its environmental problems, and frigid winters. By that time, we had two kids, Kristopher and Kimberly—and Kimberly…"

"Kimberly has special needs," I finished for him as he paused. "When she was seven months old, Wendy and Peter learned she had cerebral palsy. Her ability to function grew worse every year. By the time she was five, her mobility was severely limited, and her vision and hearing had significantly deteriorated. Peter's primary reason for jumping at the job offer in New Jersey was to better provide for her needs—better health care, schooling, and social integration—and to allow Wendy to be a full-time mother."

"I have a friend whose son was diagnosed with autism," Bernie said, "and I've seen their challenges. I'm so sorry."

Peter jumped in, saying, "At times, caring for Kimberly felt overwhelming. I was working harder than ever at sales to pay medical bills. I was as hungry to succeed for myself as I was to take care of my family. Wendy set the example for us with her faith. She believes that if you make up your mind to accomplish something for the greater good, no matter how bad the circumstances, get you will succeed."

> **If you make up your mind to accomplish something for the greater good, no matter how bad the circumstances get you will succeed.**

Peter's emotions were about to get the better of him, so once more I stepped in with an assist. "Do you have kids, Bernie?"

"Grown. I raised two boys, two years apart. They're good boys, but they live in California. I don't see them much."

Peter quickly composed himself. "My son Kristopher lives in California, too." I could tell this put new wind in Peter's sails, even though I knew he was thinking of the difficulties he'd had with Kris.

To provide context, I said, "Bernie, the most Peter and Wendy can do for Kimberly is keep her comfortable and content. Kristopher, on the other hand, had his dad's warm heart, good looks, and positive attitude. Women especially appreciate Kristopher's special gifts, depth, and caring. But one girl in particular created a situation that caused conflict. Everyone knew she was not the right girl, but Kristopher found it difficult to separate himself from her."

Peter caught the pass. "Kristopher was a good athlete. He was also sensitive, and this situation with the *needy stalker girl* became so annoying that he internalized the problem. Finally, pent up with anger, he skipped college and left for Los Angeles for a change of pace. We were stunned but could not convince him to change his mind. He was always a kind, loving brother to Kimberly, but he probably needed relief from witnessing all her suffering. The family was devastated when he up and left. We had no idea how he'd find his way out there."

"So what happened to him?" Bernie asked, now able to relate.

"He applied for a union card to act in movies. And while he waited for acting parts, he partied. This worked for him for a while, but he could have done more if he'd worked in grease like I did when I was his age and learned some discipline."

With Peter's comment, a breeze stirred through the leaves fanning the final embers of the fire. As the campsite darkened, our moods shifted as well. I thought that Bernie seemed embarrassed.

Then suddenly Peter jumped to his feet. "Enough! Maybe Bernie is bored with the conversation, and I have something special—just what the doctor ordered." He walked over to the trailer and soon reappeared with three brandy snifters.

"Do you drink Napoleon Cognac, Bernie?" Peter asked. "Here, buddy, take one."

Bernie was so riveted by Peter's insights and elegant hospitality; he apparently disregarded any fear about the dangerous proposition of hiking back to his campsite in the dark. He agreed to stay for a final drink. "I used to have this kind of whisky whenever I could afford it," Bernie replied, examining the glass.

"You know, I had a lot of bad breaks, Bernie," Peter continued. "But when I was Kristopher's age, I learned how to stay focused on work, school, and family. I was always attentive for ways to improve my life and not run away from problems. I'd still be freezing my butt off in Cleveland if it hadn't been for the courage to face challenges and recognize opportunity."

> **I'd still be freezing my butt off in Cleveland if it hadn't been for the courage to face challenges and recognize opportunity.**

Peter went off into another story I was too tired to stop. He started, "I was at a neighborhood Christmas party in Cleveland in 1968 while Wendy stayed home with the kids. One of the guests was an out-of-town friend of the host who owned an office equipment and supply company in Fairfield. It was a small company that sold mimeograph machines. At the time, I didn't even know what they were. But I saw he had a passion about growing this company. He asked if I'd be interested in coming to work for him, in sales. I looked him squarely in the eye and said, 'I don't know a thing about New Jersey or that business, but sure!' The next week he flew me to New Jersey to meet with his sales manager, his partner, and a few staff members. Two days before Christmas, he called and said, 'You start on January 21.' I was thrilled. I didn't know a typewriter ribbon from a robin's egg, yet here I was starting this new job.

"Wendy thought it was crazy, but we began packing on New Year's Day and never looked back."

"You went on blind faith?" Bernie exclaimed. Clearly feeling his cognac, he added, "Hey, wasn't that the name of a rock band?"

Peter either missed the joke or ignored it and went on unabated.

"After the factory experience and with Kimberly to care for, I had to act on my intuition even with limited knowledge. But I've been fortunate—my gut instinct was often right. I'm a perfectionist to a certain extent, but I trust my inner self. I can proceed without having every detail nailed down. It's been a thrill, and it has paid off."

> I've been fortunate—my gut instinct was often right. I'm a perfectionist but I also trust my inner self.

Peter finally lightened up. "*And* I figured out the difference between a typewriter ribbon and a robin's egg!"

"Well, I'm ... I'm ... impressed," Bernie said. "I know that a sales career is not easy. I couldn't have done that. You really had to have had your nose to the grindstone to cover your daughter's medical expenses, support your family, and still live within your means."

Enjoying my cognac with the same enthusiasm as Bernie, I heartfully agreed. "Yes, Peter may have made the cut and earned the position he'd worked so hard for, but he didn't slip into easy habits.

"Five days a week, he commuted in the dark at five-thirty in the morning to get to the office by six when many of his fellow trainees were still in bed. Once the others arrived, they avoided making sales calls by doing easier tasks. But Peter knew the only way to sell office equipment was to cold call strangers and give his pitch.

"Every day, he called at least twenty-five people. Most slammed down the phone before his second sentence. The rejection hurt, but he quickly recovered and kept working on his long-term commitment.

"Bernie, try to guess how many lunches, dinners I've done with this guy. Trust me, you now have a friend for life—and you're going to want to keep in touch with him. Someday we can all have lunch!"

"First one's on me, Bernie, since you supplied the trout tonight," Peter added.

"Great. Let's do it," Bernie said. "How do I find you?"

"He'll find you," I interrupted. "Just because he's retired doesn't mean he doesn't still scout for leads! Thank your lucky stars he has nothing to sell!"

It wasn't just the alcohol talking. Although he was retired, Peter maintained his strong sales acumen. He was still admired in the company. He rose from the training program to become one of the most accomplished printer and copier salesmen the company had ever hired.

As Bernie and Peter talked about us getting together again, I thought it was fair for Bernie to hear more about his new friend. "Peter is loyal but has a passion for justice." I broke in. "He was a great leader at work but was intense and given to heightened emotions, both good and bad. That led to an impulsivity that at times was destructive. When his son Kristopher left, he had good reason—but he inherited his dad stubbornness. They didn't talk to each other until Wendy intervened."

"That cognac is having its way with you, buddy," Peter said.

"But it's a good point," I said. "Peter and Kristopher deserve credit on this one. Kristopher's new girlfriend in California told him to trust the universe and that it would all work out—and it did. About then, Wendy told Peter to call his son, and he did."

As I laughed out loud, Peter jumped in, "I'm not proud of my stubbornness, buddy, but I am proud of my son!"

"Aw, come on, Peter. That same stubbornness is part of what got you where you are. What matters is that you and Kris now have a strong bond, and I'll bet that was one of the biggest sales pitches you ever gave!"

Peter's gaze shifted to what was left of the campfire as he pondered my statement of truth. Then he exclaimed, "Do you smoke Cubans, Bernie? I was saving these for later, but why not now?"

"It's been years but bring 'em on!"

And with that, Peter walked over and popped open the tailgate on the Cadillac SUV to retrieve the cigars.

"I struggled often, competed hard, and failed regularly," Peter said. He lit his cigar with a burning stick from the fire. "But there was one trait of mine that stood out and made people take notice. It confounded even my colleagues who'd attended the best Ivy League schools with one powerful weapon that kept bringing customers to me."

Bernie sat up straight and leaned forward. Peter exhaled a line of gray smoke that dissipated into the dark sky. "The one thing I learned that will stay with me forever," he said, flicking away the long ash at the end of his cigar, "is that you are only as good as your word. Never break it, because your word is forever written. In business, if you go back on your word, you are through."

> **The one thing I learned that will stay with me forever is that you are only as good as your word.**

Bernie was quiet. He put his lips to empty his brandy snifter. Then said, "And you're still fishing in style."

Peter flicked the remainder of his wet, well-smoked cigar into the fire. "Bernie, all good things do come to an end, but so do bad things, and in either case, there should be a contingency plan. I knew I needed to expand beyond my current way of doing things and save for a rainy day. When the money started rolling in, I still didn't let my principles weaken. I worked and saved as if the good times could come to an end at any time, like my luck was about to end. I did everything I could *not* to borrow money. You know, after I got my mortgage, I never borrowed again to buy a car or a refrigerator or a piece of furniture," he said with pride.

"I recognized too that when Kristopher left, the world's greatest spiritual leaders like Buddha and Jesus and Mohammed knew something I didn't. They made it evident that achieving greatness took sacrifice.

"So I set goals consistent with my moral values to support my achievements. I lived life to the fullest and did my best to keep my commitments to others. I was determined to pay off the mortgage so my family could live debt-free because that was what I believed to be true ownership. For years I saved and planned, and in hindsight, I'm happy I did."

Peter wasn't done.

"Bernie, I will tell you this: you can weigh the merits and risks of anything you do, but there are always unanticipated consequences. That was the case with my son. I was wrong. But I couldn't just lick my wounds like I did when the economy crashed. There is a big difference between not owing anybody and not having anybody to share what you own."

I lived life to the fullest, and I also did my best to keep my commitments to others.

By now, it was almost sunrise and the fire had burned completely out, leaving only flickering embers. It was darker than it had been all night. "I believe we've talked the night away." Peter said sleepily.

"It will be getting light and we'll need to pack up camp," I added. "Do you have something to write on? Give us your phone number, Bernie, and we'll catch up again sometime."

I got up to look for a pen in the car's glove box and heard Bernie say, "I need to find a tree."

As I turned around, I saw Bernie walking into the darkness and Peter in the opposite direction toward the camper. I waited for a while by the car with pen and paper until Peter walked over to me—but Bernie never returned.

Several hours later with our gear packed and hot coffee in hand, Peter and I decided to stop by Bernie's campsite to check on him. He was gone. We double-checked our coordinates and poked around a larger swath, but the site seemed like it was never touched by human hands.

At the same moment, our eyes focused on a crumbled-up piece of old paper partly covered in pine needles. I bent down on one knee, carefully brushed back the debris, and dug it out. Upon closer inspection, we realized it was a torn half of a U.S. Dollar Silver Certificate Star Series from 1934, no longer issued by the U.S. Treasury.

Peter and I didn't talk much on the ride home. I thought a lot about how Peter had created his own second chances and made them work. The one he cherished most was his second chance with Kristopher after their long estrangement.

I wondered, too, if Bernie also found a second chance that night by learning the true meaning of wealth—thanks to a complete stranger.

You too can use Secret Success Standards from Peter's life story like the ones below as stepping-stones to your own accomplishments:

- Be as financially self-sufficient as possible. That means avoid going into debt and pay attention to what's most important to you when making judgment calls.
- Pursue perfectionism but know what works and what doesn't. Make the necessary sacrifices while weighing the merits and risks of any offer, even if you don't have all your ducks in a row.
- Develop a moral code based on the motto that challenges are meant to be overcome without blame or excuses.

CHAPTER 5

For Richer, for Poorer

Goodness is something chosen. When a man cannot choose,
he ceases to be a man.
–Anthony Burgess

After an injury heliskiing, I decided to lay low for a while and rethink life. Encouraged by a *Palmer Holding Group* member, I took a cross-country flight to brainstorm a peace-through-prosperity initiative he hoped would vitalize the old family company, founded on integrity, accountability, and citizenship.

During what I thought would be an introspective and uneventful flight, I met a man who turned idealism into financial reward in the most unlikely of places—high-rolling Las Vegas.

Jack Thunder grew up in Nebraska when TV shows were in black-and-white and heroes stood for right over wrong. As a young boy, he studied those heroes and adopted their morals in his community where kinship, neighborliness, and self-responsibility were the norm.

Jack's affluence was founded on his unwavering ability to apply those values to current trends. He learned how to survive in business by connecting the dots and keeping his product—*flowers and love*—in the public eye. Along the way, he made lots of friends and even met one of his childhood heroes.

* * *

The gate at LAX where I waited to board a morning flight to Philadelphia was crowded. Nearby, an unusually tall, athletic, well-dressed man was having a cell-phone conversation that others could uncomfortably hear. I couldn't help but overhear him say, "Don't worry. Just chill, and you'll find a job."

Easy for him to say, I thought, assuming he was a professional athlete. *His friend wouldn't find the job of his dreams by chilling. Finding that requires stirred passions from the fire in a person's heart.*

As that thought passed, my eyes met those of another waiting passenger. It was as if she'd read my mind. Her look instantly broke my urge to interject into the conversation.

After we got the call to board the flight, I found myself seated in the same row as that same woman. She sat in the window seat, and the man in the middle appeared to be her husband. They were pleasant as we found room in the overhead bin and arranged our carry-on luggage. Once we settled, the man turned to me with an extended hand. "Hello, I'm Jack, and this is my wife, Cindy."

I recognized Cindy from the boarding area but, up close, she seemed older and more at peace. Seeing her smile for the first time implored me to reach out.

> **Seeing her smile for the first time implored me to reach out.**

"I'm Kevin," I volunteered, happy to have good neighbors for the long flight. "Were you thinking what I was thinking back at the gate?" I asked, hoping Cindy really couldn't read my mind.

"Oh, about the job? Yes, I definitely understand. Nothing in life is easy. It was quite a journey for my Jack to find his passion, too, but that's what makes life interesting."

She smiled again and looked at her husband. He was busy adjusting his shirt that he'd just pulled over his seat belt and his rather large stomach. When he looked up, his wife was gazing at me as if she'd made the assist on a hockey goal.

Jack said, "Cindy opened a door that I try to keep locked out of humility. But if you want to walk in, I'll oblige."

"I'd love to hear your story, Jack," I said with a slight reservation.

Tucking that day's copy of *The Wall Street Journal* into the seat pocket, I cynically wondered how long it would take this man to share how he made his mark in the world. I was half listening when I caught something about the weather that seemed more relevant to me.

"Raining in Philly," I said. "What did you say about thunder?"

"That's my last name," he teased. "Lightning struck once, but the thunder has been continuing for years."

He thought this was funny. To stop his awkward chuckling, I took the bit. "What do you mean?"

"It's been a long-standing joke between my wife and me, but it was as if lightning struck when I made my first million bucks. I did it in only five years without the help of coaches, agents, promoters, or fans—unlike that athlete at the gate."

> **I made my first million dollars in only five years.**

"How were you able to do it, Jack?"

"I could do it because I love to see people in happy relationships."

"What? From lightning to love?" I had to admit, I was confused but intrigued.

Jack told me he was born in Nebraska and enjoyed a middle-class childhood with down-to-earth parents, friends, and neighbors. Love was embedded in his early life experiences.

"I was fortunate to grow up in a place where weddings, baptisms, and funerals were celebrated at the only church in town near my family's home," he said.

That picture struck a chord in me, and I responded, "We were both fortunate, Jack." Now fully engaged in his message, I added, "I had a childhood filled with similar experiences."

Jack had arrived at adulthood in the early 1950s when Americans were less attached to financial outcomes and viewed work much like I did, as an opportunity to show what one is worth. At that time, mass consciousness wasn't formed by talk-show hosts. Television avoided vanity and violence, and America was basking in growing middle-class prosperity.

Flashing back, I said, "Times have really changed. Television programing is so different from shows like *Leave It to Beaver* that I'd watch on Saturday mornings."

Jack smiled approvingly and added, "My Saturday-afternoon TV shows included *The Lone Ranger* and *Roy Rogers*. That's when TV was still new. Those shows had a great influence on me."

My thoughts again drifted to the past, and my intuition told me to find out more about Jack. Maybe it was his Abe Lincoln beard, or his John Lennon eyes, but he looked honest.

> **My intuition told me to find out more about Jack.**

He turned away to help Cindy adjust her neck pillow as she was nodding off. His gentleness showed me he loved her a lot. And I could see how he regarded the lead characters of his day as role models, for they shared the same values.

When Jack turned back toward me, I was eager to hear more and switched on my perception as he spoke.

"Those old-fashioned family-based values, well, you don't see them much anymore. Me, I love my family—all of them, even the ones who are difficult, you know? Before I could drive, my grandma took me to church. And then when she couldn't drive any longer, I drove her to church. We all gave to one another as we needed. I knew all my cousins on my mom's side, my dad's side—I even knew my cousins' cousins.

"My family members were people I could count on, no matter what, no matter where I went, no matter what decisions I made. I know my mom and dad loved me unconditionally."

As the plane gained altitude, it occurred to me that things began for Jack as they did for most people—without a clue about how life would turn out. I had already learned enough about him to see that the American values of his childhood carried him through his US Air Force stint in Alaska where he met and married Cindy. After being discharged, they set off in search of warmer climates and ran out of money in Las Vegas. That's where Jack had to learn how to maneuver through a world of fast-talking wise guys and one-trick-pony businessmen.

> **They set off in search of warmer climates and ran out of money in Las Vegas.**

After hearing more details, I thought about Jack struggling to find steady work to keep alive their dream of living in sunshine. I visualized him as he sold vacuum cleaners door-to-door in Vegas's blazing summer heat. When I thought of him sitting to rest on a bus-stop bench on the Las Vegas Strip, dozing during the flight seemed unimportant. Like a child wanting to stay up past bedtime, I probed, "Well, what does one do on a hot day of no sales?"

Jack responded, "I waved off the bus driver and looked up to see a sign across the street that read Wanted: Sophisticated Salesman. So, I walked across the street to the old wooden wedding chapel."

Jack painted a vivid picture of himself carrying a large case filled with brochures and a canister vacuum he used to demonstrate suction. I smiled thinking of this stylish man next to me carrying vacuum cleaners door to door in a sweaty old shirt. As I leaned on the arm rest, I could see his eyes harden.

Jack continued, "Sweating and tired, I gathered my faith, focus, and fortitude and went into the building to ask about an interview. The owner was there, and after a short conversation, I asked for the job on the spot." He said it with steadiness in his eyes.

"I'll never forget it how the guy interrogated me. His name was Gordon Rust, and he had a gun in his pocket. He told me that a lot of cash changed hands in his business, and if I crossed him, he would get even."

"What did you do?" I quickly asked to relieve the tension.

"I smiled serenely and said, 'FINE!'"

And much like one of Jack's Saturday TV show heroes in a similar predicament, his demeanor of handling adversity with grace got him the job.

> **I smiled serenely and asked for a job.**

Eventually, Jack started managing the day-to-day operations of the chapel because his new boss had a completely different agenda.

"The next thing I knew," Jack said laughing, my new boss called me from California where he was chasing his ex-wife. He said, 'Keep the place open.' That's when I decided there must be a better way to live."

"So, what do you actually do now?" I asked, trying to cut to the chase.

"Well, it may sound simple, but I sell flowers to wedding chapels. You could say I made millions helping people in love."

Then Jack's demeanor became stern. "My friend, the definition of love comes from an idea of unconditional commitment. Most people have a very different idea about that—especially the ones who get married while in the romance stage. The way I see it, most people don't understand true love."

"Good point. We need to learn the honor and respect that defines true love."

"I wanted people to share love the way I learned it as a kid," Jack said with pride.

To this point, I'd come to know Jack Thunder's work ethic was one of perseverance and integrity. With the owner not on site, Jack kept the chapel open twenty hours a day and learned all he could. Within a few months, he was pruning flowers to beautify the event for patrons along with other romantic perks. As his hours and services increased, Cindy juggled the roles of receptionist and flower buyer.

Still curious about the essence of the man sitting next to me, I probed further, "I guess that, being in Vegas, you saw a lot of characters come through that chapel."

His laugher almost awakened Cindy.

"Willie Nelson and a few of his running mates stopped by the chapel once," he recalled. "They were playing Caesar's Palace and wanted to do a Vegas wedding for some new kid in the band. They were also having loads of fun driving around town, from the looks of them. I was sweeping the floor and feeling fatigued when they burst in the door. He asked for the owner who wasn't around, but I made Mr. Nelson feel right at home. We spent almost an hour sharing views on life, religion, and patriotism. Willie then reached into his pocket and handed me a couple of front-row tickets to his show.

"When we got to the show, all the assigned seats were taken, so we were escorted backstage to watch from there. Maybe Willie had made a mistake with the tickets, but I was shown a lot of courtesy—and being backstage was way better than the front row. I wasn't disappointed. Backstage, I got to talk to Willie one more time. This proved to be an important conversation because it established my long-standing view that *folks are just folks.*

"If my wife were awake right now, she'd back me up on that," he added. Then he adjusted Cindy's coat over her shoulders as a temporary blanket.

> **My long-standing view is that folks are just folks.**

"At first, the flower business was about giving myself personal joy. Soon I realized it could be worth my time if I made money while giving more people happiness through flowers. So, I found a wholesale supply chain and started to sell flowers at a low price. It became a win-win for everybody."

Jack smiled, leaned back, and explained how he began visiting other chapels, asking to sell flowers to their patrons.

"Were you still working as an employee at the chapel?'

"Totally right, Kevin. I needed money to build my own business, so I negotiated a sixty-forty revenue split with Gordon because I was doing all the work. Obnoxiously, he spent most of the day complaining about his wife and fighting with his girlfriend. At that time, I hadn't signed up enough flower sales with all the other chapels, so I needed to work two jobs."

Jack took a big breath, glanced at Cindy, and leaned into my shoulder.

"I must have been doing something right," he whispered. "On Valentine's Day, Cindy walked in and told me to come home because the request for flowers had gone out of control.

"I didn't have the answers then, but I soon realized we could sell enough flowers and not have to work for a morally corrupt hypocrite like Gordon Rust anymore."

> **We could sell enough flowers and not have to work for a morally corrupt hypocrite anymore.**

"How did that happen?" I asked.

"We installed point-of-purchase displays with ready bundled flowers in all the chapels in town. I even asked at casinos that had chapels. They said they didn't want a cut; they just wanted to keep their customers happy. One of the big casinos started giving my flowers away as congratulations to people applying for marriage licenses. Arranging that was a big pay day."

He took a sip from his water bottle and raised his eyebrows.

"My philosophy has always been that focusing on *keeping* your job is just standing still. I always thought I'd be a millionaire someday. Then one day I woke up and realized I'd made my first million. It happened the month before my thirty-fifth birthday, only five years after I started this business!"

"Jack Thunder," I said, "you make it sound like making a million is easy."

"No," he lurched, "making a million is about as easy as marriage itself. You start out with fun—you take a chance—then you work at it until it feels like fun again.

"Much like life with Cindy. It was love at first sight for both of us. But after a while, it took a deeper love, patience, and a lot of work. To me, love is the most important thing in my life. Flowers are just a way to show that feeling. With each bunch of flowers, I always give a silent blessing to the union of love. And now, taking a check is like being on my honeymoon every day."

We both had a good loud laugh until my business brain kicked in with a question.

"But Jack, all marriages and all businesses go through rough times, and some die just like flowers."

"Yes. I was constantly tested by the temptation of receiving 'all the kingdoms of the world'—which is not only a selfish temptation but a false promise. There was once a time when we had nothing—nothing but love for each other, that is.

"But that love encouraged us to find ways to pay the bills. Hard work, effort, sacrifice, and keeping the love alive between us are what turned my inspiration into success. I didn't stray from the path of loyalty to myself and my vision of how to run a business. Nothing could keep me from my desire to be Cindy's favorite person. Guess you could say I practiced the art of seeing how every decision made has a cause-and-effect action that could support my vision of happiness—or not," Jack concluded with a wide grin.

> **I practiced the art of seeing how every decision had a cause-and-effect action that could support my vision of happiness, fulfillment, and love.**

It was about then I realized my last pain pill was wearing off. Still eager to hear more of Jack's story, I adjusted my recently broken ankle under the seat in front of me and turned an interested eye back to my row mate.

"When I was young, I tried almost anything once to see if it would fit," Jack continued. "It's the only way to learn. My biggest lesson came from my own father. He didn't approve of my business—or Las Vegas. He thought the flower business was a 'hippie job' and he came to Vegas to tell me so. By then, we had an office with warehouse space. One day while I was sitting at my desk, Dad said, 'You can't make a living doing this. It's just a glittery Las Vegas illusion!' But this happened on a day I had a deposit bag with over twenty thousand dollars in cash to deliver to my bank.

"When I showed Dad the money, he looked me square in the eye and said, 'I've never seen that much cash in all my life!'"

> "When I showed him the money, he looked me square in the eye and said, 'I've never seen that much cash in all my life!'"

For the first time since we started talking, Jack looked younger than his years. I could see a child inside him saying, *Dad, what do you think of your son now?* Then my imaginative spell was broken by an announcement about starting the food and beverage service.

Unphased, Jack looked at me and said, "Never accept other people's limitations as your own."

He continued his story. "That visit from my father prepared me for another challenge—a media circus developed by Gordon Rust who tried to sue me for half the profits in my flower business because the business was started while I worked for him."

To quell Jack's erupting anger, I quickly responded, "I know how this kind of stuff can be difficult, but would you mind sharing more?"

"Thanks. Today, I see it as just one of those lessons we all should have on the road to wealth."

Jack put his index fingers to his temples and pressed. "It was a few days before the big Labor Day weekend when a guy came to my office. He asked if I was Jack Thunder. When I said yes, he handed me a summons to appear in court. My stomach did everything except leave my body. I'd always chosen the moral path, and here I was being sued by a con man. I was confounded that the justice system could make me look like the scoundrel due to false accusations by my former boss."

> **I was confounded that the justice system could make me look like the scoundrel due to false accusations by my former boss.**

Jack was hesitant or possibly embarrassed, but I urged him to continue. Inhaling through his nose, he then muttered, "It was nasty the way that guy came after me. He told all the other chapel owners buying my flowers that I was a thief. This guy had lots of connections. He even told the newspaper that 'flower boy would be taken away in handcuffs.' By Labor Day it had become a big media event."

Jack wiped his brow with his sleeve.

"When a TV reporter showed up at my door, I couldn't speak. Then the words came from my soul, and I made it clear that my job all along was to run the chapel. It's a job I did better than the owner, and I loved to see people joined in matrimony. The flowers were a personal gift to them. When I started selling flowers as a business, everyone including Gordon Rust signed a contract to receive and pay for flowers. He had no idea I'd make so much money."

"Fair enough," I replied.

"In the end, this case was thrown out of court, but I feared it would damage my good reputation. As it turned out, most people already knew what a scoundrel my former boss was. They wanted to do even more business with me because, while I ran his chapel, I improved the reputation of the industry and that was good for all owners.

"Within eighteen months after the scandal, my business almost doubled—and even my dad was impressed."

Although Jack's story fascinated me, my neck was hurting from being turned toward him, so I reached for my newspaper in the seat pocket. Still curious, though, I asked, "Your business plan was always flowers?"

"Yes, but the reward wasn't always money. Every transaction has reward in some sense if you can look for a greater good."

He turned again to check on Cindy before continuing. "One time, I had to decide to go up against a competitor who had set up shop a few blocks away and was using all kinds of bells, whistles, and come-ons to shut me down. I know he was financed by Gordon Rust, but I decided to honor my history and do what I did best. In effect, I did nothing to counter him, but the result was to strengthen our reputation as the kindest, most-loving service in town.

"Through that time, Cindy worried enough for both of us, but I stayed strong even though I felt terrified. Her facing that fear probably kept us from having kids."

He paused and let out a big sigh.

"But our legacy ties in with the memories we've given people. Thanks to us, each married couple was surrounded by beautiful flowers as a symbol of their love, even if their marriages didn't survive. The money I've made is probably a lot less than those who work in the divorce industry, but I dream of the day when the reverse is true."

At this point, Jack turned away from me and put his head on Cindy's shoulder. He was clearly tired of talking, and I needed a break, too.

I finally opened the newspaper and my eyes scanned the day's stories. Still, I kept thinking about how Jack worked every day to increase his marketing knowledge and better identify and then separate primary from peripheral issues. This helped him focus on good decision-making when facing adversity and stiff competition. He had learned through old-fashioned on-the-job education. You might say he earned a blue-collar doctorate in the flower business. And making people happy made him rich.

It occurred to me that Jack's actions and philosophy could work for almost anyone building a business or networking relationships for potential dividends. The floral business, like most others, survives on promotions. Jack Thunder knew he needed to always keep that in mind. Letting people know who you are and what your business does is essential to success. Jack regarded it as *nothing ventured, nothing gained* so he expanded his promotions to chapels, casinos, and conventions. He built his reputation through honest communication.

> **Letting people know who you are and what your business does is essential to success.**

Hearing Jack's story and thinking it over during that long flight inspired me. His journey demonstrated axioms that apply to all people in any economy or political system. Indeed, his Secret Success Standards came up like water from an underground spring within him.

The millions of species on earth all depend on each other in some divine way. Humanity is merely individuals all wanting the same thing but finding it in different ways. Everybody sells something, even if it's not for money. Jack's unique business had a strong root in the human need for love in a most intimate way.

In fact, Jack believed his service was a mission of love that he may not have been able to define. But he kept up the practice and went the extra mile in managing employees and navigating issues. Being comfortable with a multitude of transactions—and knowing all of them had to be based on integrity or love—added to his successful business model.

When the captain announced the flight's final descent into Philadelphia, I turned to Jack and asked, "Why'd you fly from L.A. to Philly?"

By now Jack, was sitting straight up in his chair and Cindy was tucking her pillow into the bag under her seat.

"We are visiting Cindy's brother-in-law Charlie and his daughters for a few days," Jack replied. "We've done it every summer since Cindy's sister died in 2009."

"I'm sorry. How old are the kids?"

"Older now, and they're doing well. In fact, the oldest daughter just announced her engagement. They wanted to get married in Lake Tahoe over the December holidays. We will be there for that event and are taking care of all the details—not just the flowers," he smiled.

"The other daughter just graduated from college in interior design, and I plan to pick her brain on remodeling some of my stores in Las Vegas and Reno," he added.

As we landed, I marveled at this man and his story about treating others the way he wished to be treated. Jack was in the flower business and even though love was the reason, he honed material characteristics to master his business and reach his purest potential.

> **Jack had honed material characteristics to master his business and reach his purest potential.**

The plane came to a stop on the runway and the captain announced the plane had to wait for a gate before we could disembark. "Keep your seatbelt fastened," we heard over the loudspeaker. "The bad weather in Boston has caused some backups here."

"Bad weather gives me time to tell you another story about how lightning struck with thunder," Jack said with excitement.

"It's another good story," Cindy chimed in, "if you can stand one more."

"Tell me," I replied, loosening my seatbelt in anticipation of a leg stretch.

"I remember standing at the door of Gordon Rust's chapel feeling discouraged and realizing I was being used and abused by a not-so-nice man," he said sheepishly. "All of a sudden, a cab pulled up and a guy in cool sunglasses jumped out. He had a silver bullet pinned to his lapel.

"I recognized him as Clayton Moore, the actor who played the Lone Ranger. The Lone Ranger was one of my childhood heroes!"

Again, seeing the little boy in Jack's eyes, I asked, "What did you say?"

"I asked him, 'Are you lost? This is a wedding chapel, not a place for Lone Rangers.' At that point, he knew I recognized him, and he laughed. Then he said, 'I'm not lost, but my bride-to-be might be.' So, I put him in my car and drove him to the condo where she was staying with friends. Their friends hadn't returned to pick her up because their car had a flat tire. Knowing she was fine and roadside assistance had completed the repair, Mr. Moore and I went on to make final preparations, which included picking up a lot of extra roses.

"Just as we finished at the chapel, the future Mrs. Moore showed up stunningly dressed, ready to be wed. At that point trying to be a good chapel manager, I asked him if he wanted us to play *The Wedding March* at the end of the ceremony.

"Clayton Moore jumped up and said, 'No! I want The William Tell Overture.' Knowing that was the TV show's theme song, I asked, "With the Hi-Ho, Silver tagline, right?"

"Yes." I felt like a kid again—but only for a second because his bride-to-be said, 'Clayton, will you grow up?'"

"But men being boys, I whispered something into Clayton's ear. And after the ceremony as he and his new wife drove off down the Las Vegas Strip in a silver Cadillac, he looked back and shouted, 'Hi-Ho, Silver!'"

> **Driving off in a silver Cadillac, he looked back and shouted, "Hi-Ho, Silver!"**

Smiling from ear to ear, I looked at Cindy and said, "I see why you like that story so much." Then turning back to Jack, I asked, "What's next for you? Are you planning to retire?"

"From business in a few years, but I'm not retiring from life. I recognize the reality of who I am, and I've learned to have faith in myself as a part of something greater. I'll always want to quantify my passion for helping people in love. So, I'll go on with the company in a minor capacity, but I'll let the young ones take center stage in the business."

As the seatbelt sign turned off, Cindy kissed him on the hand, showing her genuine love for her husband.

> **I've had to recognize the reality of who I am, and I've learned to have faith in myself as a part of something greater.**

That night on my way to dinner, I recalled Jack's parting words to me: "We live in a great country, this America. Here, you can live free and be anything you want to be."

Yes, thanks to Jack's heroes—and to heroes like Jack himself—others will know they, too, can fall asleep with a dream and awaken with a purpose. Any dream can come true.

You too can use Secret Success Standards from Jack's life story like the ones below as stepping-stones to your own accomplishments:

- Forming a vision and committing to it with abundant faith helps you see your success. Take reasonable risks, even if the information you have seems incomplete. That's where faith comes in.
- Employ goodwill, perseverance, and old-fashioned honesty. Showing goodwill to others builds toward building the reputation you want.
- Caring and thoughtfulness also go a long way, no matter who you're working with. Move through situations, even day-to-day activities, without ever uttering unkind words.

CHAPTER 6

Inner Compass

As darkness falls, I can hear them telling stories.
The scent of cigarettes. There's danger in the air.
—**Alejandro Escovedo**

It makes no difference who came before whom. All Americans are immigrants. Everyone can trace their starting roots in this county—even the *homo sapiens* who crossed the Bering Strait during an ice age 14,000 years ago. Because of this, we are all part of an immigration story.

It was my love of wild horses, that brought me to know a person who lived life like the conquistadors, whose adventures he had read about during childhood. As an adult, his stamina inspired him to overcome judgment and cultivate a reputation as an astute learner with sheer determination. His reward was respect from his new community, peace for his family, and wealth from his own enterprise.

I met this extraordinary man through my friend Mark, an immigration lawyer who lived in my neighborhood. Mark was a founding member of an equestrian program for at-risk kids.

We both shared admiration for horses and children because of similarities in the beautiful boundless spirits of both. We got to know each other while working hands-on helping kids in a dusty corral at a horse rescue ranch near Spur Cross Canyon.

* * *

Early one Monday on the way out to the ranch, in what had become a routine ride in Mark's F-150 pickup truck, he seemed more thoughtful than usual. Placing his coffee in the holder between us, he coyly turned to me and said, "Hope you're chipper this morning because I have something to share."

"Is it about work? Because if so, it's not a workday!" I said lightheartedly as I gulped from my triple espresso.

"This isn't really work, at least not for me," he said with a mocking, flippant tone. "I helped someone years ago when I lived in LA, and we stayed in touch. He happens to be downtown this week for a convention. Knowing how much you enjoy people's stories; I think you'll be interested in meeting him."

Our drive to the ranch in those early hours with the rising sun behind us was peaceful, never filled with too much conversation. We usually reflected separately to prepare for something we enjoyed. Today I wondered what made Mark feel the need to talk about this man.

"Is your old friend staying near the convention center?" I asked, taking another sip of coffee for some conversational strength. "I need to be downtown a few times this week. Who is this guy, anyway?"

"I'm taking him to dinner on Wednesday night," Mark responded almost on cue, although I pretended not to notice. "Can you make it? I don't think you'll regret it."

Wishing for our usual solitude, I consented. We spoke briefly about the logistics, tinkered with our cell phones, and agreed on a plan. It became quiet again and I gazed out the passenger window.

<Insert a light bulb division element here>

A sweet, earthy smell filled the cab, announcing the proximity to our destination. As we took a sharp right onto a rural road, the wheels hit dirt and the bumping rhythm of the ride shook Mark's lips loose once again.

"His name used to be Andrés, but he adopted the American version Drew when he got to California. After growing up in poverty and coming to this country in the most unusual circumstances, Andrés—I mean Drew—has overcome enormous obstacles, not just geographically but in businesses." That's what makes him so unique."

Mark explained that Drew's grandfather, Pablo, had come to the States in 1960 with his son, Esteban, and worked legally as a *bracero*—a farm worker in the California fields. When the bracero program ended in 1964, Pablo went back to Mexico, but his son Esteban stayed as an undocumented laborer in Los Angeles because he loved the United States. His work ethic and personal habits kept him under the radar of the immigration officials.

> **Esteban's work ethic and personal habits kept him under the radar of the immigration officials.**

"Wow, can you imagine?" I said. "Our families have been in the United States for generations. I've completely lost my perspective on what their struggles might have been when they were new to this country. So, what happened to Esteban?"

"Back home in Mexico, his family carried on without him, but his sister, Jordana, built her eldest brother up into a mythic character. She made a big effort to stay in touch with him, and he encouraged her dream of coming to the United States."

Mark fumbled in his pocket and lit up a non-filtered Camel. "I told you to cut out that crap out." I said, rolling down the window.

"My last one," Mark said indignantly, looking me squarely in the eye and stepping harder on the gas.

"You likely won't recall that, in 1986, another change in immigration law granted people like Esteban citizenship. By then, Jordana had married a man in her little town in Mexico and had two sons, Drew and another boy named Pedro who kept his given Mexican name. Jordana was permitted to get visas for all of them as soon as her brother Esteban was granted citizenship that year."

Mark took a long puff and then smashed the cigarette into the clean ashtray. He said, "The sad thing was Drew's grandfather Pablo died before Jordana had the visas in her hand."

I was genuinely fascinated, especially after reading recent news about stronger border controls.

"So, without the legal lingo, Mark, how did this family get into the United States?" I asked.

> "How did Jordana's family get into the United States?" I asked.

Another hard right into the ranch entrance and Mark slowed the truck to a crawl, patted his pocket for his cigarettes, and mused, "Well, that's where things got complicated. Jordana's family was wealthier than most in her town but still very poor. Once their paperwork came through, she arranged for cheap transportation with a coyote."

"Don't coyotes smuggle people without papers?"

"Usually in this case. The arrangement was for the guy to take them to the border where they could cross legally. But things went terribly wrong, and they were put in a van with several people crossing illegally. Instead of being taken to a border crossing, they were dumped in the desert under cover of night and left to find their own way."

With that, Mark came to a full stop.

"Enough for now. We need to focus on kids and horses. It looks like we have a crowded corral. You can get the rest of the story from Andrés—I mean Drew—when we all meet."

Before jumping out of the truck, we confirmed arrangements for dinner with Drew, and that was the last we spoke of him. When I returned home later that day, I went online to read more about immigration and became excited to meet Mark's friend to find out more.

The Greek restaurant was crowded when I arrived. Both Mark and Drew were already waiting for me at a table. "Hey," I said reaching out to shake the hand of a handsome, dark-haired man with a five o'clock shadow surrounding his huge smile.

Drew wasted no time. Above the loud chatter, he said, "Mark told me about how you like to hear stories!"

"It's nice to meet you." I said, startled by his quickness.

"How do you like our city?" I asked, wondering what Mark had told him about me.

"It compares well to Los Angeles where I first lived and Orlando, which is my home now," he said.

I took my seat facing Drew and said, "Mark told me that you came into the country legally, but your situation wasn't all that easy to understand. I'd like to know more about how you crossed the border and how America welcomed you and your family."

"It's a sad story," he began, "because I watched my father die in the desert. I was only seven."

> "It's a sad story," Drew began, "because I watched my father die in the desert. I was only seven."

"I'm sorry..."

"It was traumatic for my family, to say the least, but I got to where I am today because of his sacrifice, and I feel eternally blessed."

"Achievement rarely comes without sacrifice. Can you share what happened?" I asked.

"Unknowingly, my mother had hired someone to drive us north to the border, and he turned out to be a coyote. He was not trustworthy and dumped us in the desert. We had no idea how to get to California. It was hot, and we had little water. My father gave what little water he had to my mom, me, and my brother, and we didn't know he wasn't drinking at all.

"Our shoes baked on the ground as we walked, and when our water ran out, I felt light-headed. We were lost, but at one point I remember having a very strong feeling about the direction we needed to go. When I turned to check on my parents, I saw my father grab my mother's hand. He took a shallow breath and said, *'Brújula interna.'* To me it meant something about following my internal compass. Those were the last words he spoke.

"With a slight gasp, he lay down and died right before our eyes. It was so hot our tears were not wet."

> In a shallow breath, my father said something about following my brújula interna—my internal compass.
> Those were the last words he spoke.

Drew took a moment to gain his composure as Mark glanced compassionately at me.

"We stayed the whole night at the spot where Pedro and I buried my dad in a shallow grave. The next thing I remember was feeling the warm sunrise and hearing the sound of racing engines drowning out the sobs of my crying mother.

"From a distance, I saw a swirling dust cloud and four-wheel drive SUVs. When they were close enough, I tried to translate the emblem but was interrupted by a megaphone that squawked in Spanish: 'US Border Patrol. Stay where you are.'

"I had no idea where the officers were or why they were so hostel toward us. We had visas, but they took us to a facility that was a cross between a jail and a hospital. My mother somehow mustered the strength to keep us going until it got all worked out. During the process, they also contacted my uncle Esteban who was living outside of Los Angeles. We were told we needed to move in with him."

Mark smiled warmly and interjected, "Drew was just a kid when his uncle Esteban came to me for legal help. That's how we met."

"Yeah, my mom was a mess. My uncle wanted to adopt us, but my mom was stubborn. Esteban helped her find a job, and my brother and I went to school. But life was difficult. We didn't speak much English. Uncle Esteban helped us learn, and I picked it up fast. English was hard for my mom."

"Jordana was beautiful," Mark said with admiration.

"Was?" I asked. "Don't tell me you lost your mom, too!"

Don't tell me you lost your mom, too!

"Not in that sense. My uncle found her a job cooking for a farmer who owned lots of land. His company hired migrant workers at very low wages along with rooms in his trailer camp. Mom worked at a central kitchen and delivered food to the workers. That's how she met Ron, my stepfather. He managed operations."

"So, you were in Los Angeles, your uncle took you in, your mom was suddenly a single working mother, and you and your brothers had to navigate school and the English language."

"Exactly. I liked school once I learned the language. Math came easy to me—because I like numbers too. My favorite class was history. I read a lot of books on my own about Father Kino and the conquistadors from Spain."

> **I read a lot of books on my own about Father Kino and the conquistadors from Spain.**

Mark attempted to keep a big sip of wine completely in his mouth as he added, "Drew helped his brother get through school, and he stepped up at an early age to help his mother. Right, Drew?"

"I did. What saved me was that my mom made friends with a guy who worked on the farm and took care of horses. She took us out to his ranch on weekends, and my brother and I got to ride and learn to take care of those magnificent animals. Everything about my regular life was difficult—until I was at that ranch with those horses. Aside from my early experiences in Mexico, my best memories are tied to horses and how free and empowered I felt when riding them. The regal history of how horses helped build America is often overlooked, but they were a backbone of work and companionship in early America.

"When I got into high school, I thought it was my job to be like the great American horses and serve my family. My uncle was good to us, but he was married by then, and the living situation became strained. That's when I changed my name from Andrés to Drew, short for Andrew. I thought we should have American names and Andrew was my favorite apostle. He was the first apostle of Jesus.

"My brother and mom didn't agree with my name change. But I didn't want to be judged as an immigrant. I wanted to feel like I fit in, and I was willing to work hard and do everything I could to prove myself."

> **I didn't want to be judged as an immigrant. I wanted to feel like I fit in.**

I was riveted by the determination I saw as I watched Drew's eyes. "That must have been difficult—to fit in and still serve your family."

"It was!" he said tightening his sight.

"I used to have to take care of my brother while Mom worked until we were old enough to work in the fields after school. The summer I turned eighteen, my mom married Ron, and my life changed again."

Mark wiped his chin with a closed fist and added, "I was present at their wedding. I remember how unhappy you were, Drew. But I must admit, Jordana and Ron were a nice match for each other."

Drew turned swiftly to me and said, "Ron was the great-great-grandson of a Mississippi slave, and he was no stranger to hard work. He had risen through the ranks to run the entire operation for the farm owner."

"Drew, correct me if I'm wrong," Mark said, "but I think you can thank Ron for teaching you about the farm business—even though you were angry he moved your mom east after the farm owner passed away."

"That's true. Ron was a good teacher. I learned from him like I learned in school. And when the farmer died, I was the one who explained the situation to the migrant workers. They had no loyalty to the man who paid them paltry wages, and they showed no regret when they were told they had to move on because the land was sold to developers."

"Developers?" I said, not very surprised. "There's a song about that—something about paving paradise to put in a parking lot."

"It was kind of funny, though. Things were evolving. Mom, Ron, and my brother Pedro moved to Orlando, Florida, because Ron had a job offer. They all wanted to start a new life.

"Everybody moved on except me. As they drove away, Mom told me to follow my *brújula interna*. All I could think was, 'Two parents gone and now I'm on my own.' After I said good-bye to them, Uncle Esteban helped me again. I lived with him and his wife for two more years to get my own start."

> As they drove away, Mom told me to follow my brújula interna. All I could think was, 'Two parents gone and now I'm on my own.'

"So, what did you do?" I asked with fascination, realizing I hadn't even touched my food.

"I still had to work, man! So I found a job as a dishwasher surrounded by other Mexicans in a peer group littered with bad examples."

Drew pounded his fist on the table. "Several dishwashers were engaged in illegal activities to make more money. I didn't want that. Instead, I wanted honest work, and understood the need to go to college. I asked the restaurant owner how I could become better educated."

Drew pounded the table again this time more gently.

"He hadn't even finished high school himself, but he kindly gave me a recommendation for a job at his friend's landscape company."

Done eating dinner and on his second glass of wine, Mark continued the story. He said that, within a few weeks, Drew was spending his days landscaping yards in some of the nicest neighborhoods in LA.

Then Drew picked up the conversational slack. "One day, as the landscape truck moved along Santa Monica Boulevard, I was standing in the back with the equipment. Grass and leaf bits were blowing all around me, and I felt a sense of freedom like never before.

"Even though I was just part of a landscape crew, I made all kinds of new friends. The first affluent person I met was a dentist who happened to be African American. I saw him and said, 'Wow! This is how I want to live.' Because of him, I wanted to be a dentist.

"A year later, I met another guy who was doing well financially. When I found out he was an insurance agent, I said, 'Oh great. I want to be an insurance agent.'"

Drew laughed and held his head as he said, "For me, it wasn't necessarily the profession but the lifestyle I wanted!"

> **For me, it wasn't necessarily the profession but the lifestyle I wanted!**

We all had a good laugh and, after gaining his composure, Drew continued. "I was living with my uncle, saving money, and taking night classes at the community college. I soon found a roommate so we could share an apartment. On weekends, I went to the beach and learned how to relax a little with my college friends, not my fellow landscapers."

"So, college opened some doors for you," I affirmed.

"My classes were all right, but I especially loved running alone on the beach. A friend who ran track races suggested I try out for the college track team. This helped me understand how to train and compete in the actual long run—and in life, too. I ran in life like I was winning every day, even before I had a penny to my name."

> **I ran in life like I was winning every day, even before I had a penny to my name.**

Mark was clearly overjoyed at how easy the two of us were getting on at this dinner. He said, "Drew's friends from the beach knew he was working hard to make money and stay in school. He had the tools he needed to accomplish his goals and had a personal power that caused people to gravitate toward his innovative thinking.

"But it started to take its toll."

"Yeah," Drew shuddered. "Thanks for reminding me, Mark. Ugh.

"Although the landscaping job was a blessing, due to the hard work, I could barely stay awake in school. I also started missing late-night and weekend social time, which was not acceptable. So I quit landscaping and got a part-time job in a restaurant again, this time not as a dishwasher but as a waiter. Those two years helped me develop a long-range perspective. I learned to identify ways to turn around problems at work and among friends."

> **I learned to identify ways to turn around problems at work and among friends.**

I could see Mark was proud of himself for the introduction as he happily added, "And then, after a year and a half, Drew accepted a partial scholarship to a four-year college."

"True that," Drew added. "I was to finish my last two years of college as a real student, but it was a culture shock. It was an extremely difficult transition for me."

"Yes," Mark said, "but you accepted the challenge and learned to compete against yourself for your own approval. You increased in confidence and pride, and you used your work ethic to stay focused on success."

Mark waived down a waiter who had paused to tune in to the conversation. Drew took the opportunity to bend closer to me. "It took guts, but I went directly to the divisional supervisor of the restaurant and asked for a management position. I got the job, quit school, and was on fire! I loved the business lifestyle and managing the bottom line. I met a lot of entrepreneurs who sold products to restaurants, and I got a taste of what they saw as success."

Mark sipped his fresh glass of wine. "Here's some wine for thought, I mean food for thought—Drew used that management position as a sort of college education."

"You mean managing a restaurant and learning at the same time," I asked Drew, who was still leaning into the table.

"Well, my heart was really still in the outdoors," he replied leaning back and grasping his hands behind his head.

"There was nothing like the feeling of being free and boundless that I'd had around the horses. So, once I saved a little money and learned all I could, I left the restaurant and went back to the owner of the landscape company. I made him a deal."

"A deal!" I elbowed Mark. "You really did learn quickly!"

> **There was nothing like the feeling of being free and boundless that I'd had around the horses.**

"You're right Kevin!" Mark shot back with an even harder jab to my ribs. "The kid got his job back and even negotiated a management training role—but this is where the story came full circle.

"The company Drew worked for used to do the landscape maintenance at the office park where I work. One day, he was working on the grounds at my office and I recognized him. There he was—Esteban's nephew, almost grown!

"We talked for a long time, and he asked me questions about how to start his own company. He told me he could see how setting up systems would make the difference in how and where the landscape crew was dispatched on different days for different duties."

"Seems like he was a natural." I interjected.

"Yes. He and I talked several times, and soon Drew was basically running the company as a foreman. He stopped at nothing to do a job well, whether it was pruning bougainvillea, driving the crew, or interacting with property owners."

"Mark's right," Drew said, pushing back from the table to signal we were about done with dinner. "But I still wanted my own business. Deep down, I wanted to do it my way from scratch and manifest my own vision of independence."

Knowing well the difficulties of realizing the dream of entrepreneurship, I wanted details. "Did you manage to get a loan?"

"The banks were not interested in taking a chance on me, so I had to be creative. First, I saved up to buy a used truck, lawnmower, and some tools. Then I went back to see the owner at the restaurant where I had been a dishwasher. I asked him for a loan. He wouldn't give me any money, but he arranged my first contract—weekly maintenance on the restaurant's property.

"Then he hired me to work at his home and told his friends and neighbors, and the contracts started to come my way. I got great joy from the mix of labor, creativity, and business. It seemed to be the same kind of feeling I had when first seeing the Pacific Ocean. I felt connected to an infinite kind of intelligence that guided me to the next level of achievement."

I reflected on what Drew said, rubbing my fingers on the empty glass between my hands and nodding in agreement.

"It occurs to me that your subconscious sparked the power to create," I said. "As your ideas became more creative, your tasks became more complicated, but you started to understand the freedom and responsibility of your own livelihood, right?"

A huge smile swept across Drew's face that lit up his deep brown eyes. Then he said, "People who help guys like me are few and far between. The owner helped me help myself. Pretty soon, restaurant patrons were asking for my services. It was built-in advertising. Within twelve months, I was putting in six days a week and had achieved success that was harmonious with my nature. But I made one big mistake. I lacked confidence to do the accounting."

"Drew's self-reliance and confidence kept him building a team with high moral commitment. He was the kind of guy I'd hire at the law firm—someone who could manage events for different outcomes," Mark said supportively.

"There was only one problem. He was careless in protecting his ultimate goal of ownership. Accounting was a tough lesson."

> **Drew's self-reliance and confidence kept him building a team with high moral commitment.**

Mark looked at Drew as a father consoling a son who had lost his dog. "He collected all the revenue from clients but turned it over to the restaurant bookkeeper who paid expenses, employees, and presumably gave Drew the rest—but let's just say the bookkeeper made more than Drew!"

"Wow!" I said. "How did you change that one, Drew?"

"Change has a way of following me. Soon after I discovered I'd been taken advantage of, life brought me another challenge. Ron had become ill. So, I leaned into adversity, and that took me away from California."

Fascinated by his resilience, as I wasted no time asking, "What happened next?"

Drew was not a man who stood on circumstances, and he quickly replied, "One of the things about being on my own was that I was lonely. I thought about my family a lot. My uncle was always kind to me, but I missed my mom and brother. Even Ron. My mom and Ron had a baby, Alesha, and in all the years, I had never even seen her. The other interesting thing was my mom finally changed her name from Jordana to Joan, and she took Ron's last name—Jefferson."

Then Drew rolled his eyes to heaven. "Anyway, Ron's health was deteriorating, and my mom was overburdened. My own brother didn't even call to tell me—Alesha did. She was only twelve."

> **My own brother didn't even call to tell me—Alesha did. She was only twelve.**

As Drew spoke, I noticed that Mark was gazing down at the table. "What did you think of all this, Mark?"

Slowly lifting his head, Mark jerked 90 degrees toward Drew to explain. "He was being asked to give up what he had worked so hard to build and go East to take care of the family that left him behind. The trip alone would eat up a third of what he had saved."

Drew intervened. "For days, I prayed—prayed for the strength to not go back. But I couldn't fight it any longer. My inner compass was pointing to family."

"So, I worked out a fair partnership agreement with my best employee—well, not so fair to me," Drew smirked. "He would take over the books and the business in the short term and eventually buy me out a little at a time. With that done, I split to Orlando to help my family."

Mark spoke up again. "Drew didn't know Ron well. Before he married his mother, Ron was just another guy who had authority. Drew had never recognized his stepfather's ingenious ability to invent something without depending on sources outside of himself.

"Much like Drew, Ron found ways to invent gadgets and get a job done on the farm without a lot of fanfare. When Ron moved to Orlando, he partnered in a successful handyman business and eventually become sole owner. But not long after, he got sick. When Drew arrived, it was a tense situation. Ron was sick, Pedro had no interest in helping, and all the work and burden fell on his mother."

Nodding incessantly, Drew pushed into the storytelling. "I needed to come up with a plan to bind our family. Life is unfair. Sometimes the good guys lose. But I believe it's up to us to change the dynamic in our own part of the universe."

> **Life is unfair. Sometimes the good guys lose. But I believe it's up to us to change the dynamic in our own part of the universe.**

Drew then paused, so Mark added, "Then Drew's half-sister, Alesha, started hanging with the wrong crowd. She was an innocent beauty with skin as smooth as obsidian and eyes deep and pure like her mother's. She shares the same intelligence as this guy right next to me."

This time Drew jabbed Mark with an elbow, saying, "I told her I wasn't going to take anything from her father, but I would collaborate with him to get a benefit for all concerned. To me, shifting Ron's business to landscaping made sense because, over time, we could integrate backwards into the existing client base with added skills."

"So you persuaded Alesha and your mom to change the business, but what about your brother Pedro?" I asked.

"I had a conversation with Pedro one day as he was on the way out the front door. He had no intention of listening, and just before the door slammed, I shouted, 'I'm committed to making this endeavor beneficial for you as well—however that happens!'"

> **I'm committed to making this endeavor beneficial for you as well, Pedro—however that happens!**

Mark pushed his wine away and reached for a glass of water dripping with condensation. Then he continued the story.

"Drew realized that taking the helm of Ron's handyman business would prove to be a lot harder than simply taking an immediate pay cut. But he was committed to placing his own financial and personal well-being aside to make his mother, brother, and stepsister his priority. Still, he wasn't aware he was on his way to capturing his true desire. As I told you Kevin, Drew has a remarkable story."

For the first time all night, Drew seemed humble. He was breathing at a shallow pace and his eye contact became random. "Mark has been my silent champion," he said with gratitude.

"When I got to Florida," Drew continued, "my duties doubled, and my income became nonexistent. Pedro was on the company payroll as a mechanic but showed up only when asked to do a job and on every Friday to collect his check. He preferred to hang with his posse. To light his fuse, I showed him he could be with his friends all day using the landscape company concept. Pedro had a ton of friends he could recruit as laborers or simply as contact people. They would discover underserved niches in the community for minority-owned businesses like ours."

Drew's breath became deeper and his initial excitement resonated in his voice. "In landscape services, other businesses don't mind partnering with minority-owned firms as long as we understand the decision-making criteria and try to be the best. After analyzing Ron's business, I knew that a landscaping service would be an easy sell to his clients. That way, I could transition the handyman business into landscaping services for homeowners and their businesses, just like I did in LA. I knew my expertise running a successful landscaping business would outpace the profits of the handyman side of the business." Then with a laugh, Drew finished. "And since Pedro liked being the boss, he could run his homeboys."

> **And since Pedro like being the boss, he could run his homeboys.**

Again, like a dad proud of a son, Mark added, "Within the year, Drew was proved correct. Revenue from Ron's handyman clients easily transitioned to landscaping at an increasingly rapid rate. Pedro was running crews and hiring his friends while Alesha helped her mother with the bookkeeping. Out of respect, Ron, who could no longer do any labor, was given the title of CEO."

"I called a family meeting every Monday night," Drew continued. "It was the highlight of Ron's week and gave a boost to his deteriorating health. During one of the weekly meetings, we decided to transition the few remaining handyman clients to a friend of Ron's and focus our energy entirely on landscaping services."

The evening had flown by, and I had to admit Mark was right. Drew was an inspiration. He used his intelligence and resources each time life presented him with a challenge. But there was one more thing I needed to know.

"Drew, how did you expand so far into the Orlando market once you got your family on board with landscaping services?"

"I called on the largest homeowners' associations and municipalities in Orlando and asked for their landscaping contracts. Within four weeks, I signed three big contracts—two upscale condominiums and a public park."

"What about capital?"

"Ha! The eternal question," he said, putting his finger in the air.

"I needed new landscaping equipment to support the new contracts, but financial doors were being slammed in my face. Then one hot and humid day when I lacked courage, I stopped at a discount movie house to get out of the heat and catch a matinee. I paid little attention to the show as I worried about my failure. But when I walked out, I kept hearing a line from the movie *2001: A Space Odyssey*, an oldie but goodie. I was destined to see that movie that day."

> ### I was destined to see that movie [2001: A Space Odyssey] that day.

Mark smiled and fumbled with his iPhone. "Here, listen to this YouTube, Kevin." He pressed play.

"Good afternoon, gentlemen. I am a HAL 9000 computer. My instructor taught me to sing a song. If you'd like to hear it, I can sing it to you. It's called 'Daisy.' ... 'Daisy, Daisy, give me your answer do. I'm half crazy—'"

Mark stopped the video.

"After leaving the movie, that song drove me half-crazy," Drew said with exhaustion. "Then I realized the letters H-A-L—the name for the ruby-eyed computer—that were all one letter away from I-B-M, the giant computer company. To me, that meant I needed to try a variation in how to raise money. So, I revisited the people who wanted me to buy their landscape equipment, showed them the new contracts, and persuaded them to lease it at a weekly rate instead of selling it. After that, the rest is history."

We laughed hysterically and Mark was first to catch his composure. "That's why Drew's in town this week. He's attending the Landscape Equipment trade show."

"One of these years, I'd like to be a speaker there," Drew added shyly.

I have no doubt you will," I agreed, feeling his conviction. "Where are you now with the business?"

> **"My biggest problem running the company has always been management," said Drew.**

"My biggest problem running the company has always been management. All five family partners had different ideas on what I should do with my time and efforts. One wanted to expand too fast. One wanted to spend profits instead of reinvesting them into the business.

"After a year and a half of squabbling about money and other decisions, I knew it would be easier for me to run the business on my own. So, I worked out a deal. I'd pay each of the family partners a buyout fee over time until the transfer of ownership was complete. They could continue to work for me or find a job they liked better. That meant I had to pick up the management slack, but it also meant I could expand intelligently.

"Truthfully, they were thrilled not to be working for me. Still, I found myself starting over once again."

It was clear that despite all of his skills, Drew understood the meaning of bootstrapping and had pulled himself up from nothing more than once to make his dream a reality.

> **Drew had pulled himself up from nothing more than once to make his dream a reality.**

It was Drew's time to shine in front of his longtime friend. "In my industry, it's difficult for customers to distinguish superior services if they're not performed consistently. We consistently performed very well. In addition, I scrutinized every single job from the moment it started until it finished. I used a business process called the Four Cs: customer-service, consistency, computer technology, and competitive pricing, and I've been tested to the limit, but I achieved!"

Mark was clearly proud of his young friend.

"Let me tell you that Drew took his operation to the multimillion-dollar level using flexibility, patience, and tactical savvy. He controlled his own destiny by watching how business was done in America and adopted programs from the best corporations for this traditional, labor-intensive industry."

Like a preacher on a pulpit, Mark continued, "While his competitors were doing a good job mowing, raking, and pruning, he did a better job hiring, training, and ensuring his systems provided critical points of differentiation from his competition. His new company became one of the fastest growing in the state of Florida. It received accolades from many community and business organizations, including an award for minority business owner of the year. Drew is too humble to tell you that, but that's why he keeps me around as his friend."

Mark did a double take and then said about Drew, "And here's something else he won't tell you: this man gives back to the community in an unusual way."

> **This man Drew gives back to the community in an unusual way.**

Drew tried to protest. "Mark, you don't have to—"

"No, last story of the evening. Remember how Drew said that in his childhood, the only time he felt free was when he got to spend time with horses on the farm?"

"Yes," I said. "I too feel a fondness for those beautiful animals."

Drew had started tapping his finger on the table. Then he said, "When I got to a certain point in my business, I was invited to go horseback riding with a woman I'd met at the chamber of commerce. While on the ride, she told me of a dream she'd had about getting kids who were abused paired up with horses. That way, they could learn about safety and connection. She believed these animals could teach lessons about life in gentler ways than these kids had been taught before. I knew it was a great idea because horses had done exactly that for me.

"So, she and I joined forces to form a charity that has grown tremendously over the last eight years. It's where I spend most of my time. When you come to Orlando, I'll take you out to the stables. You can ride, or you can just watch the kids engage with the horses—I'm very proud of them."

Mark turned slowly toward me and, with an "I told you so" smile, he said, "This kid is something else, and I guess you figured out where the inspiration for our local equestrian program came from."

This time I jabbed Mark in the ribs as he handed the waiter his credit card. "Thanks for the invitation, Drew," I said. "I hope to visit one day soon."

Drew and I both thanked Mark for dinner and the introduction. With that, we stood up to leave and suddenly realized the formerly busy dining room had emptied—all except for kitchen workers. They had positioned themselves at a table close enough to hear the tale from the last three men in the restaurant. They heard about how one of their own diligently pursued self-education, kept self-confidence intact, and gained traction every day.

As I drove home, I thought about how Drew's winning attitude and work ethic allowed him to stay focused on his dream and not fret over change or harbor anger over bad breaks. Rather, he embraced opportunities and trained himself to take charge of his own life. Consequently, he has proudly built a large fortune and earned great respect as a mainstay in his community.

You too can use Secret Success Standards from Drew's life story like the ones below as stepping-stones to your own accomplishments:

- Let family and education be your core drivers to success. Make the most of family values, education, and determination. Enjoy uncertainty. Regard problems as changes that open doors.
- Follow your inner compass. See events, issues, and people from a higher perspective, and train not for a specific event but for a lifetime of winning. Don't let negativity from colleagues, friends, or family members plant self-doubt in your mind.
- Create and rely on a long-range vision for your life. Know that you can lose everything except what you've learned.

CHAPTER 7

Myself in Others

The surfing life, I discovered against the backdrop of the city,
is a venerable one.
—**Ed Thompson**

While visiting in Los Angeles one summer, I invited my niece Brooke to lunch. She was bright, beautiful, and had a law degree but was employed as a retail clerk. She was making even less than I did as a bartender while working my way through graduate school, and her dad was getting concerned.

We were joined that day by two cousins, Matthew and Damon, whom I'd met years earlier during a surfing retreat for corporate executives in San Clemente, home of slow crumbly cobblestone reef break. Matthew and Damon's course had taught the group much, encouraging even the most accomplished execs in our assemblage to reach the next business level.

I hoped they could likewise encourage Brooke to see the silver lining in her employment cloud—to face fears, envision potential outcomes, find her true earning potential—and perhaps even pick up a few surfing tips.

* * *

The two cousins had spent their childhood together—their mothers were close loving sisters. Although Matthew and Damon were not siblings, an interesting contrast marked their relationship. With the respect and honor taught to them in childhood, they worked through their differences and learned the value of both the judgment and nonjudgment of people.

They chose to go to the same college and while living on campus together, eventually were drawn into a business venture. The introverted Matthew had created an innovative software program for businesses, and the extroverted Damon sold it. Operating this business gave them an income while they earned their bachelor's degrees. One of them saved the money, the other spent it on beer, dates, and parties.

As adults, both men retained some of the characteristics they'd shown in childhood. Damon was confident and boisterous; Matthew was rather antisocial and pensive. When I showed up for lunch that day, I knew my niece Brooke—with her tall slender body, natural blond hair, and subtle personality—would make them open to genuinely sharing information about their two very different lifestyles.

The hostess seated us at a table where we had a view of the Pacific. We could watch gentle waves breaking under the lingering marine layer and noticed two surfers on the shore gazing at the ocean.

"Looks like conditions just aren't right for them today," I remarked awkwardly to my niece, whom I hadn't seen in quite a while.

Like her dad, Brooke wasted no time and got right to business. "As for me, Uncle Kevin. I can't even get a toe into the job market. Guess I was born at the wrong time."

Spreading my fingers over hers to compensate for my years of not being supportive, I said, "Earning a diploma from the College of

William and Mary's law school is never the wrong timing. The job market today is just unusually tight ever since the mortgage crisis."

I tried to be matter-of-fact about it that day, but this lunch took place three years *after* the housing market crash that brought the U.S. economy to its knees. Although the recession had officially ended in 2009, the Western world was entering a second more insidious downturn within an ongoing, economic contraction that history would coin The Great Recession. This was happening despite record high results on Wall Street.

"I'm afraid the economy has hiccupped, Brooke, but perhaps our guests will offer insights based on their experience of leaving college in the mid-1990s, a time with its own economic struggles," I said. Just as I finished expressing this thought, I spotted Damon and Matthew walking to our table.

> **Perhaps our guests will offer insights based on their experience of leaving college in the mid-1990s, a time with its own economic struggles.**

"Hi, you two," Damon said as he extended his hand to me and then to Brooke. "What's for lunch today besides a view of that pathetic wave action?"

"Hello, hello," Matthew said, shyly trying not to make eye contact as he reached out his hand.

"Have a seat. And thank you for joining Brooke and me."

As they studied the menus and pretended not to listen, I shared their biographies with my niece to seed the upcoming conversation. Then with menus on the table and eyes back on Brooke, I looked to Mathew, then to Brooke, and said, "Technology might be considered Matthew's second language."

"Really?" Brooke said with surprise.

Matthew was nonplussed.

"He took to the family computer before he could talk in complete sentences," I said with my familiar cynical tone. "When he was a sophomore in college, he created an end-to-end supply-chain-management software platform that small companies could use to track inventory and process sales results."

Still hesitant to look at Brooke, Mathew followed with, "The software was scalable and could be customized for various companies."

"It was a brilliant piece of work and well timed for business conditions back then," I added, "but it would have gone nowhere without …"

"Damon!" Damon said, finishing my sentence.

"Yes, you did have the brains for business," I acquiesced, looking back at him. But by then, Damon was focused on Brooke who was happy to receive his glance.

Vying for some of the attention, Mathew jumped back in. "My cousin had a lemonade stand during the summers in his childhood. Every purchaser of lemonade also garnered five cents off on the second glass. A bit of a child prodigy, he knew how to pique the interest of a buyer."

With that, Matthew stood up. "I'm going to wash my hands. Please order for me—I'll have the California Caesar salad with grilled salmon."

> A bit of a child prodigy, Damon knew how to pique the interest of a buyer.

Damon again turned to Brooke. I could tell she had already bought into his charm. "Your uncle told me you're wondering what your career path will be. I'm not sure we can help you, but if a good story is worth anything, you'll probably take something away from our song-and-dance routine today," he said in a playful tone of voice.

Unintentionally batting her eyelashes, Brooke searched for words. "Uh, I was told you two caught the early waves of new technologies. If I could design software like your cousin, I'd be employable. But my training as a lawyer is to move two parties from a place of disagreement to a resolution."

To break the spell, I piped in. "It's not any different for you, kid. Just seize a good idea and run with it. You have to figure out a new, better way to play the game you've been trained to play."

"Well, the new, better way won't be electronic," she replied." At that point, Matthew returned.

"Did you tell her that creativity and innovation will always be good for the economy?" Matthew asked without hesitation.

Brooke smiled coyly. "We were waiting for your wisdom on that truth, Matthew."

Then Damon sat back. "Matthew, tell the young lady more of your story, and I'll add to it when necessary."

Mathew fiddled with his collar and scooted closer to the edge of his chair. "You may have just come out of college into a world that feels unstable but let me tell you what was going on when I was in college.

"In 1994, I was at UC Irvine struggling with mundane tasks of academia. Early that year, thirty Palestinians were massacred in Hebron. One of them was a family member of a good friend of mine. My grief over his death put me into a depression, and I felt haunted by worldwide unrest.

"Also, we had an earthquake registering six point eight on the Richter scale. Orange County was forced into the largest municipal bankruptcy filing to date. And if all that wasn't enough, a strike by Major League Baseball players forced my favorite pastime to be called off for the season. Times were bleak—as bleak as they are now."

> **Times were as bleak—as bleak as they are now.**

Damon was clearly having a hard time being second fiddle, so he took an opportunity to step into the conversation, saying, "Matthew was feeling low, but that didn't stop him. I saw how closely he was paying attention. He wasn't particularly popular because he spent so much time in his head. I even had to keep pulling him away from programming to get him to have fun with our friends!"

"Yes, Brooke, I was—and still am—rather awkward in social settings. But my friend and cousin always provided me with a measure of balance."

"Are you kidding, Matthew? Your sense of self-reliance and responsibility had been developed to the point of mastery by high school. It kept you out of the trouble I got into," Damon said with a touch of pride.

"Surprised you never needed a lawyer, Damon," Brooke teased. "Remember, you're supposed to give me hope and encouragement. So far, it's been no better than those flat, sloppy waves!"

Damon's head tilted back to laugh, and the ocean breeze lifted a shock of bleach-blond hair, illuminating it in the sunlight. Brooke's eyes locked onto him.

Trying to snap herself out of a dream, she blurted, "You guys seem like total opposites. Yet you are relatives, friends, and previous business partners. How did that work for you—I mean doing business in college?"

Matthew and Damon looked at each to see who would answer. Then Matthew popped in and said, "Damon had fun comparing me to the autistic savant character in the movie *Rain Man*. He kept forcing me to get out of my head, out of my room, and into risky behaviors."

> **Damon kept forcing me to get out of my head, out of my room, and into risky behavior.**

"That was mean!" Brooke whispered in an approving voice.

Damon swiftly replied, "Matthew does some things well and other things as if he has no clue. It's borderline embarrassing to be with him sometimes. Other times, I'm amazed at his clairvoyance." Brooke could hear the smile in Damon's voice.

"Matthew's personal life has been something to witness," he continued. "His dorm room had no visible floor space because his laid-out laundry had five or six stages. If he wore a piece of clothing one time, it came off next to the bed. As an item got dirtier and dirtier from subsequent wearings, it got closer to the hamper until finally it was deemed dirty enough to be washed."

"That's true," Matthew said, "but smart people like me select skills to use based on the results they want most at the time. My laser focus, frugality, and trust in Damon to sell my product is what led us to become millionaires—and why he can now live his life's passion in the water."

Intrigued, Brooke questioned, "What *is* your passion, Damon? I'm curious!"

He smiled his California smile. "Now that I'm done working with corporate America, I'm a surf instructor. I've always loved the beach, and Matthew's genius made it possible for me to fund the lifestyle of my dreams."

Attempting to make Mathew feel special, Brooke laid her hand on his shoulder to move a little closer and sighed, "Why did you do that for your darn cousin?"

"Damon has social skills that are off-the-charts excellent," Matthew exhaled. "I created a product Damon eventually sold to a company that took the program and ran with it. Because of that, we crossed into big-time financial success."

At that point, our food arrived, and we all took a pause. "Mind if I say a silent blessing before we begin?" Matthew asked as he bowed his head, glancing at me during the motion.

"Go ahead, Matthew," I replied.

"We feel blessed to be here today with Brooke and Kevin, and thank you for all our gifts, amen."

As we raised our forks, it was my turn to talk to my niece. "Brooke, Matthew makes it sound like success was effortless, but I know it wasn't easy. He was persistent, and he approached new things with focused enthusiasm while ignoring the rules so he could search for unique resolutions. Nerdy or not, he found a vehicle to stimulate his core talent early on that made for a rare experience."

> **Nerdy or not, Matthew found a vehicle to stimulate his core talent early on.**

Damon jumped in to help. "Brooke, you're young, yet Matthew was younger than you when he hit on his passion. Age isn't a factor in finding your divine skill or talent. I've read that author James Michener advocated that people *not* make a career decision at least until the age of thirty. Some people don't find greatness until they reach the winter of their lives. Colonel Sanders began Kentucky Fried Chicken in his sixties, and Harriet Doerr published her first novel, *Stones for Ibarra*, when she was seventy-four years old."

I was about to mention that her book went on to win the year's National Book Award for a first work of fiction, but the boys were showing more interest in Brooke than this conversation.

"You're actively seeking enlightenment, I can tell, Brooke," Matthew said, testing the waters. "I did the same thing. You can find it as long as you stay on your path and are open to it when it appears. As you discover your talent, it takes time to manifest it. So first, prioritize and select the skills you'll need to get the best results."

> ## Prioritize and select the skills you'll need to get the best results.

"For me," Matthew continued, "it was enough to create that software, but then I realized it had no usefulness. That's when my cousin stepped in to take the software further. It was his persistence and social grace that became the matching piece of the puzzle."

"He's right," I said. "Matthew created; Damon sold. Both were working with a unique product and playing to their unique strengths."

The summer breeze softened, the conversation took on a lighter tone, and we focused on our meals. Brooke was first to break the silence. "I see you two are still friends, but what happened after college? There must have been some bumps in the road for you."

"Matthew hated to work on routine things, so he'd build complex theoretical solutions, but he was too dreamy to get them launched. I figured out how we could make more than two grand a month for work that took twelve hours a week," Damon said with glee.

"When Matthew described the software's potential to me," Damon continued, "I got on the road to find buyers. That's when the money started rolling in. The money from sales allowed us to spend the rest of our college time taking road trips and doing rock climbing.

"Matthew also spent a lot of time playing video games, maybe hundreds of hours, but it made him happy."

"Ah, happiness," I said, eager to pipe in. "It doesn't always get its fair due. But how did you learn to sell Matthew's software program? Was it a tough sell?"

"I learned from Matthew—of all people!" Damon responded. "Despite the chaos in his dorm room, he had a small but perfect place in front of his computer where he could tap into his natural talent and block out outside noise. His computer became a college education unto itself."

> **Matthew had a small but perfect place in front of his computer where he could tap into his natural talent.**

Mathew became excited to speak. "Here's the thing: computers are structured on a system of branching logic. That means a programmer says, 'If this happens, then you'll do this, and if it doesn't, you'll do that.' I used that idea to research companies Damon could cold call to tell them how the software could solve their problems. And from there—plus a lot of hard work—the magic just happened."

As another waiter arrived to refill our water glasses, Brooke pushed her salad to the center of the table. She had finished her meal but not her questions.

"Matthew, I see the dynamic between you two, and I can understand how you both made it work before you were even on the career track. Tell me about one of your experiences that might help me navigate my own situation."

Matthew was happy to answer Brooke's empowering question. "The kind of logic you have to use when creating a computer program is something you can focus on, even if you have a degree in law or history or anything," he said as he fiddled with his napkin. "You can program yourself like a computer to look at a particular challenge and envision all the potential outcomes. From there, you can visualize what plans you would make to address them."

Brooke's face relaxed as if she finally understood. "You synchronize your knowledge to improve a specific niche that others didn't see or even know exists," she summarized.

Not to be outdone, Damon sailed in. "I pitched business-to-business service companies to provide a high-quality, dependable, useful data system at a low price that eliminated the middle man."

Trying to keep the conversation on track, I wanted to clarify for Brooke that although the cousins' software business had begun when they were college students, they continued after leaving. "Matthew's genius kept things going after graduation, right Damon?"

"Right, Kevin. It took a while to realize we'd done well with this," Damon admitted. "We were concerned that the business could bankrupt us, so we lived on $25,000 a year at a time when we were bringing in more than $250,000. After about four years of doing that, we realized we'd amassed over a million dollars. It was a shock to us."

> **We realized we'd amassed over a million dollars.
> It was a shock to us.**

Damon, whose mood was almost always bold, became sanguine as he looked out to the ocean. "Soon after making that first million, we parted ways, and I tried my hand at the corporate life. Some parts worked well, some were a struggle.

"During that time, I met a group of young executives who started big technology companies. They got together every week to surf and talk strategy. These young executives were a big help to me in ironing out business issues.

"However, I realized the biggest thrill for me happened when we were waiting for waves and discussing cutting-edge ideas. That's when I decided to start a business of hosting surf retreats.

"Today, I teach corporate-executive types how to catch and hold a wave—not only the ocean kind but the consumer kind, too. I know I've learned more from my students than they've learned from me."

> **I know I've learned more from my students than they've learned from me.**

Impressed by his own wittiness, Damon continued. "Matthew, on the other hand, stayed on with the company that bought our software and ran its IT department. He and I stayed in touch after we parted—mostly because he liked relying on my free advice about managing the sales process."

With that, we all laughed so loudly that people at the nearby tables looked askance. Then the waiter noticed our empty plates. "May I offer the dessert menu?" he asked.

"Sure," I replied. "Bring me a slice of your famous chocolate-marshmallow cake with a side of rocky road ice cream and a few spoons. Oh yeah, I'll have an espresso, too."

"Any other coffees?"

The others shook their heads no, and then Damon said with a smile, "Rocky road ice cream! Brooke, we have a secret to tell you."

"About ice cream?"

"No, rocks."

"Oh yeah," Matthew quickly responded. "Rocks. Thanks to Damon, one of the secrets of our success is that we started rock climbing together in high school. It's a story Damon loves to tell because, as you can see, I do not look like a rock climber."

I piped in. "You've heard the phrase 'what you resist, persists,' haven't you, Brooke?"

"Mm-hmm. Did Matthew resist you, Damon?"

"Of course, but from the moment I first saw rock climbers on TV in high school, I wanted to do it. Matthew thought I was out of my mind when I asked him to try it with me. He was so opposed to it that I needed to keep escalating the challenge and cajoling him. Finally, he accepted."

"How'd you get him to do it, Damon?" Brooke asked as she leaned closer and wiggled to the end of her chair. Her body language indicated this was the entire reason she'd agreed to attend today's lunch.

> **Her body language indicated this was the entire reason she'd agreed to attend today's lunch.**

"I first tried to get Matthew to catch my enthusiasm," Damon explained. "When that didn't work, I knew I had to appeal to his intellect. So, I bought some equipment and asked him to help me figure out how it worked. Then I introduced him to my friend JT, who loved the sport. JT had a sister, Stephanie, who'd caught Matthew's eye at school, but he was afraid to talk to her.

"To make a long story short, Matthew's first time on the ropes eventually led him to tying the knot. I used the promise of having Steph drive us to the location to bribe him to go with me and JT.

We climbed, we enjoyed, and Steph and Matthew dated after that. They got married two years after graduation."

Matthew smiled contently to hear Damon retell this story.

"Brooke, you women can be strong motivators for us men." Damon said with a wink.

Brooke smiled softly and asked, "Stephanie must be special. What does she do?"

"She's a pharmacist."

"Well, she must be smart."

"She is," Damon said. "She married Matthew! But really, rock climbing is the secret to Matthew's success now—not marriage or chemistry. His rock climbing has helped expand the talents he's used in business."

> **Matthew's rock climbing has helped expand the talents he's used in business.**

Excited about expressing his deep love for Stephanie, Matthew jumped into the conversation. "I was terrified of two things," he said, "climbing up a straight surface and asking Steph for a date. For me, rock climbing bridged both factors: fear and possibility. Starting a life-changing undertaking and climbing a cliff that holds the possibility of instant death aren't much different. Both involve similar risks and similar processes. Each requires painstaking control and testing what to do ahead of time. Understanding this helped me expand the reach of my soul to adapt to changing environments—in business and in romance."

Brooke's smile turned a bit more feline as she asked Damon the same question. "What about you? What woman or women changed your life?"

"I can't wait to hear this," I said, pushing my chair onto its back two legs. I was ready to enjoy the challenging spot in which Damon was now sitting.

As Damon squirmed about how to share his love life with beautiful Brooke, I began to tune out. I knew he had left a trail of broken hearts but had also walked the path of the brokenhearted. When it came to love, he was still learning about his destiny.

As a student in his surf school a few years earlier, I'd learned he finally succeeded in love and life by mentally reviewing possibilities and dangers, and then he chose the path that felt right. That gave providence a chance to serve its purpose.

Yes, riding waves turned out to be an excellent teacher for both me and Damon. His formula seemed mundane on the surface, but when combined with discipline and an ability to implement, I've found it has worked well. Something I hoped Brooke would soon learn.

With that thought, I rejoined the conversation about taking risks.

As I refocused on the group, Damon still had the floor. "Although risk can never be completely removed in business, surfing, or rock climbing, it can be reduced. Rock-climbing techniques include letting go of a length of rope and locking off at specific times for a controlled fall. This is part of ascending any challenge.

"Indeed, learning to fall is just as important as any other aspect of upwardly moving good performance. Aversion to risk and fear of failure are the leading reasons people don't pursue their dreams; it's why they never grow rich."

> **Indeed, learning to fall is just as important as any other aspect of good performance.**

Finally, it was Matthew's turn to be the critic and sage. "I've seen some parts of Damon's life that are completely loose—to the point that I've wondered how he gets anything done. He likes people and will drop what he's doing to go with a group of fun seekers on a moment's notice. His spontaneity is usually an asset, but it can be a detriment when he extends his willingness to do things with friends too far. He has difficulty saying no to play and fun. And that's why I think Damon's the perfect person to run a school that teaches people surf skills because he prefers interactive learning. He gets how people learn through play.

"But I admit that when he was in an occupation that required him to wear a wool suit, not a wetsuit, and was doing presentations and closings, he excelled there too. I feel safe roping up on a hundred-foot wall with Damon. I like the way he ties knots and follows safety precautions. And surfing with him, especially when the waves are rough, is a fantastic experience. He clearly puts a different part of his brain to work."

"Thanks, cousin," Damon said humbly glowing from the praise he'd just heard.

"But I want to add something. As for communication—in sales, scaling, or surfing—it's extremely important to express ideas correctly and succinctly as you convey what you believe to be the truth," Damon explained. "That's how you make things look easy to your friends, clients, and partners in sports, business, and in life."

Things instantly got quiet as they tucked their spoons into my tantalizing dessert. Brooke was the first to ask the next question. "How'd you get into surfing, Damon? And Matthew, what's better for you: surfing or rock climbing?"

Uncharacteristically, Matthew replied first. "When we were in college, I followed Damon into the water—just like I'd followed him up the rocks in high school, although in high school, a woman wasn't involved. Seriously, I wanted to learn to surf because Damon made it seem so easy and fun."

> **Seriously, I wanted to learn to surf because Damon made it seem so easy and fun.**

Damon couldn't help but vie for Brooke's attention by saying, "Matthew didn't resist the waves like he did the rocks. I started surfing, and one day, Matthew joined me. I had to teach him how to do it, but it was fun for both of us. He helped me know that I have the talent to teach people."

Matthew would not be upstaged in front of Brooke, so he added, "In college, when our emotional funds fell short, Damon drew on his *stay active and keep learning* philosophy. He chose surfing as the action that improved both of our lives."

Damon then turned directly to Brooke. "After I taught Matthew to surf, we went at times when I knew he was feeling empty. Surfing filled him back up—renewed his spirit. In a similar way, we tend to approach business like surfing and surfing like business. That is, a strong surfer can make it look easy to ride a challenging wave. Get it?"

"I do," Brooke said, feeling totally engaged in the company of the two men.

"By the way, when can I take a few surf lessons?" she asked.

"Wait, wait, wait a minute," I said. "We'll all go out one day soon when we celebrate good news of Brooke's next job and how her timing and preparation met opportunity."

Brooke's girlish manner began to fade. "When I couldn't get a summer internship at a law firm, I mailed out a lot of résumés and cover letters, but—well, I don't know what to do next. What would you guys do if you were me?"

Matthew jumped in first again and said, "Lawyers solve problems. And people will always have problems. Figure out who has the most problems and start there. Maybe you could work at a legal-aid clinic or in the court system to build your experience."

"And let's get you in the water someday, too!" Damon added. "I'll teach you to surf—then you can ride the world. For now, your old uncle needs to join us in the water after lunch. I think the surf is flat enough for us to bring him back without a ding."

As lunch ended, we all hugged a long good-bye. I privately hoped my niece was opening to the endless possibilities for her success—now that she understood it doesn't begin only with intellectual or physical effort.

With that, Damon and I headed for the beach.

<Insert a light bulb division element here>

As the sun set in the distance, I sat next to Damon waiting for a decent wave. He was on his performance board designed to shred while I was on my old-school long board.

"What did you mean when you told Brooke you learned more from your surf students than they did from you?" I asked.

"The stories!" Damon shouted, loud enough for me to hear over the breaking waves. "Like last year, when I met a retired sporting-goods company executive. He once worked for a stock brokerage firm. The guy told me he'd been among several candidates picked to advance into the Executive Suite. The scrutiny he went through was intense. He was put before panels of senior executives who questioned, observed, and tested him. When he was asked about his hobbies, he said he played golf and tennis, but he especially loved to surf. One arrogant top-level guy laughed and asked him how surfing could have anything to do with helping his career path. The committee quickly turned cold to the poor guy. It was like he got caught in the undertow."

Damon paddled closer. "He still had to attend a cocktail event the evening of the interview, even though he felt flattened like waves in a sea breeze. He ended up talking with a new member of the senior executive committee about the disastrous interview.

He was able to make his point about how sports such as surfing build character, stamina, balance, and connectivity to the force of nature. And he said it loud enough for the others to hear."

> **Sports such as surfing build character, stamina, balance, and connectivity to the force of nature.**

"He didn't get the job," Damon continued, "but this loss opened him up to earning a million dollars that year. He ended up leaving the industry because he was offered a million-dollar pay package with a sporting goods company. From there, he spent years working hard using his core beliefs and vesting in the company's stock-option plan. He retired rich and young."

By now, Damon had drifted so close that our boards were almost knocking in the choppy water.

"Years later," Damon continued unphased, "the executives who had asked the question in this guy's assessment interview were among those who bankrupted the brokerage firm. In effect, it was the same top execs who disrespected the candidate because he loved surfing who failed the interview."

As Damon laid his chest square on the board to paddle away, he turned his head toward me to say, "See that gorgeous house on the cliff overlooking the beach? The guy I was talking about bought that house out of foreclosure from one of those jerks who failed him in his interview."

Looking at the massive, stunning house on the hill, I imagined my Brooke someday catching the right wave with both her head and her heart. I saw her solving problems by bringing together unrelated facts and turning them into understandings that bridge fears and possibilities.

The sound of Damon's voice broke my train of thought. "Paddle, man, paddle! Here comes one, your first real challenge of the day!"

You too can use **Secret Success Standards** from Mathew's and Damon's life story like the ones below as stepping-stones to your own accomplishments:

- Focus with laser precision to create what you want, leaning on your strengths while depending on trial and error. Learn the intricacies that can create efficiencies—and make the effort look easy.

- Walk the fine line between control and letting go. Discern which operational tasks benefit you and which can be left unattended without undue risk.

- Bring together seemingly unrelated facts into information that will benefit your cause. Do so with an intention to determine how technology can enhance both your personal and professional effectiveness.

CHAPTER 8

Dancing to a Heartbeat

For fear your grace should fall.
—**David Bowie**

In sound economic models, people add value and there is a direct benefit. Corresponding reward usually is proportionate to what is provided. Problems arise when people steal reward through power. In the public sector, it's an easy place to infiltrate a hierarchy and force reward without giving adequate return, which is why if possible, I have little to do with politicians.

However in the past, when asked to share my expertise with a governor, I dutifully accepted. First, because I believe success is not when you can command services from others, but when you can render service unselfishly. Second, my background was quintessential for turning the tide during that problematic economic period.

My goal was to add tangible improvement for all citizens. The task was not as simple. I needed to gather twelve visionary business leaders who could craft comprehensive strategies that would advance job creation, attract new businesses, and add economic diversity to the state.

As in all daunting initiatives ego and power came into play. Yet, below the surface I discovered a more beautiful story of humility, discipline, and self-validation. It came by way of a female executive in a group dominated by men. Her name was Jane and she far exceeded my greatest expectations.

* * *

During my committee tenure over those long months, I was surrounded by some of the best market-oriented thinkers and doers from many industries and sectors. We assembled to leverage our executive talents and experiences, but none had come so far in her personal and professional development as Jane Lesser.

Jane came from modest beginnings and often doubted herself in her younger days. Her desire to reach the next level had regularly been extinguished. By reframing situations to manage insecurities and act outside her comfort zone, she pulled herself up by her bootstraps and maintained her integrity, turning defeats into opportunities. This formula eventually made her millions of dollars.

What I learned from Jane furthered my understanding of how emotional intelligence leads to decision-making processes that improve the quality of life. She, at the very least, doubled the value of what I received from my volunteer efforts.

Jane Lesser was called "*Little* Lesser" by her bookish brother. He was the size of a tree compared to his sister, ten years to a day younger. The two enjoyed a close relationship while growing up on their dairy farm in Wisconsin. Jane's parents were salt-of-the-earth folks who worked hard to meet the family's basic needs.

Farmers for generations, they were proud to be self-sufficient. For them, the outside world was a distant distraction.

Throughout her education, the long quiet bus rides past rolling green pastures under storybook-blue skies put space between Jane's morning and evening farm chores and the adventure of school. She liked farm life and was a good student. But mostly she loved attending an extracurricular dance class. Jane was an introvert by nature, but music touched something deep inside her that opened her into another world of rhythm and motion.

> **Music touched something deep inside of Jane that opened her into another world of rhythm and motion.**

The first time I met Jane, I was deep in my task of putting together this economic think tank. Finding the best thinkers to fill the tank was not easy. I looked for people who knew the problems and possibilities of the current business landscape and had the time and wisdom to think beyond old ways and make changes through new ideas. Finding candidates and calling them to action was taking more effort than I'd expected, and I was becoming discouraged.

By the time I interviewed Jane, I had filled eleven of the committee's twelve openings and was behind schedule. By then, I was considering going with a team of only eleven. The day she showed up, I wasn't in the best of moods. When the office door opened, this petite, well-dressed woman came in, stopped, and looked straight at me. Then she turned around and took a few steps out the door. I was stunned, confused . . . and interested.

> **This petite, well-dressed woman came into my office, stopped, and looked straight at me. Then she turned around and took a few steps out the door.**

When she finally did sit down, I noticed how her tailored navy-blue dress with gold buttons complemented her dark blonde hair done up in a conservative twist. Her pearl necklace, earrings, and her glasses came into view as she bent down to put her leather briefcase in front of her chair.

"Hi," she said, raising her head.

"Hi," I responded, still not sure what I was getting myself into. "Are you sure you're in the right place?"

"Oh, do you mean it's not common for people to walk into your office and out again? I suppose that was quite strange." She smiled. "Usually I'm very straightforward, but I have a quirk."

"Walking into interview appointments twice?" I smiled back.

"Not just interviews," she explained, looking to the floor. "Music comforts me, and when I'm a little nervous, I hear music in my head. I keep the beat with each step. If I enter a room and the music is still playing, I walk out for a minute to let the song finish. Then the anxiety is over."

It was as if a light shown through the window, illuminating her shiny gold blazer buttons. Instantly distracted by her comments, I needed to collect my thoughts.

"I guess that's a good way to begin an interview—unusual but no doubt effective," I mustered.

"You know it is! When I was young, I discovered dance. Most days after school between second grade and senior year of high school, I danced—for fun and as a creative outlet."

Making a check sign in the air, she finished, "And now you don't have to ask me how I spend my leisure time."

We both laughed. I felt immensely relieved from my own anxiety of not only meeting her, but from my angst over completing the team. She too had clearly overcome her jitters and disarmed me in the process.

"Good," I said. "Now tell me about your company."

"My husband and I are in the business of medical transportation—ambulances for emergencies and vans for non-emergencies. We both had experience in that space, so we started our own company and grew an outstanding revenue stream. We've navigated vendor contracts, and we want to keep expanding. The population is aging, and more people need this service."

"That's true. It must be some business. I'm familiar with your company's reputation and your eye to the future of that industry. That's precisely why I thought you'd have good ideas to contribute to our think tank."

But on a deeper level, I was curious about her hobby and the person who was unlike any of the other eleven on the board.

> **I was curious about her hobby and the person who was unlike any of the other eleven on the board.**

"What part of the country are you from? Where'd you grow up?"

"Wisconsin. I grew up on a dairy farm," she said leaning back in her chair. "It was my job to muck the stalls from the time I was about seven until I turned eighteen. When my brother left home, it was all up to me."

"Unpleasant work." I said, sensing a sadness in her voice.

"That was easy compared to the other things I've lived through. I've often thought back on it when I'm facing tough problems on the job. So much starts in childhood, doesn't it?"

"Seems to."

The hallow I'd imagined had long faded, and she seemed to speak to me from a distance farther than in front of my desk. I invited Jane to continue her story.

"Farm life was isolating. Like my family members, I'm an introvert at heart. What saved me was my first dance class. Two teachers who were married to each other taught it. I thought they were so romantic, and I loved listening to music—given we had no music at home, just the farm reports on the radio. Moving to music made me feel more alive than doing anything else.

"When I was fifteen, during every spare minute, I practiced a dance routine for the school's talent show in late spring. Just before I went on stage, my music tape malfunctioned. I had no music to dance to. There I was, on stage waiting. The adult running the sound system just shrugged. When I realized my music wasn't going to happen, I danced anyway by listening to the music in my head and moving to the melody. I got a standing ovation. That experience changed my life forever."

"If I wasn't so exhausted now, I'd stand right now to applaud you," I teased, elated by her tenacity.

"Aww!" she sighed, then continued her story. "They applauded me. Some of them even stood up. Not for my dance talent but probably because I was strong in the face of unforeseen circumstances—but I was a mess of disappointment."

"But you stayed engaged. Most people wouldn't have been bold enough to go on with the show without any assistance."

"My parents ran the farm without any assistance, so the idea of going on in the face of adversity had been embedded in me."

> **The idea of going on in the face of adversity had been embedded in me.**

I recognized a truth and forwardness in Jane that I admired.

"So what motivates you now, Jane?"

"I haven't always been focused. There was a time when work was even fun and easy—like parts of my childhood. When I was seven years old, I picked strawberries and earned fifty cents a crate. When I was a bit older, I had a job making ice cream parfaits. That was all fun and didn't feel like work."

She was starting to confuse me, but I could sense an innate power in this woman. It made me wonder how it all connected to her personality.

"You had some positive work experiences. Most people take for granted the cooperation between working and a payoff. Your awareness of that connection makes you especially valuable to the group."

"Thanks for the compliment. When looking back, I see the one thing that got me connected to life was dance. More than anything, it taught me discipline in how I expressed myself creatively. It also gave me a taste for competition—I so wanted to win that talent show, although I didn't even come close," she laughed. "But without learning about competition early on, I'd be nothing. Without motivation and focus, I'd still be on the farm doing the same chores over and over with little room for creative self-expression. I was so lucky to find dance."

At this point in the conversation, I knew I would ask Jane to be part of the Private Enterprise Council, and it seemed she could tell. So I picked up her curriculum vitae, handed it to her, and said, "Choose something on this and tell me about it."

"Really? That's not a question." She said this with confident abandon, confirming my previous thought. She then glanced at the document and put it back down on my desk with a thud. "You know, I'm older than I look, and that means I've had a lot of life experience that's not in my CV."

Then her lips parted slightly as she held back a smile. "You're going to ask me to fill that last spot in this group, aren't you? And you know, I think it's a good thing. We're going to be friends. I want to help this great state I live in and have a lot to contribute.

And I have a child, so as my legacy, I want to improve the business landscape here."

> **We're going to be friends. I want to help this great state I live in and have a lot to contribute.**

Clearly, she had me figured out, but I didn't confirm her suspicions so I could maintain at least *some* decorum. "Good, but let's keep this going," I responded. "Please tell me about your education."

She bent down to grab the briefcase from in front of her feet and then put it on her lap. I knew the action was unrelated to anything she was about to say, but I appreciated her gesture to keep the formality.

Tapping the leather bag, she mused, "To get away from the farm, I went to community college in Monroe after high school for a certification as an emergency medical technician. I also got a job working as an intern for the ambulance company. It was some crazy hectic schedule."

She looked behind her at the door she had entered twice, tilted her head, and said, "One day, I went on a call with the team and found a forty-five-year-old farmer dead of heart failure. It was the first time I'd seen death up close. It was life changing! Have you seen someone die?"

"Uh, no. Animals, but not people. I do know seeing birth and death are hugely important to understanding our journey in life. Please tell me how that experience affected you so much."

"I knew I had to put my personal priorities in place. I was only nineteen. Most people don't get a wakeup call that early. What changed me was, first, watching how the professionals worked in emergency situations—doing everything they could to bring him back, to comforting the family while maintaining their professionalism and not getting involved on a personal level."

Bowing her head toward the briefcase in her lap, she finished, "I was involved in the drama that day, even though I did all the things I was taught and had practiced. After it was over, I was scared. I missed my family, felt bad for that dead man and his family, and cried. It wasn't unlike when I felt distraught after the talent show, but I had to hold my feelings inside."

> "I was involved in the drama, even though I did all the things I was taught and had practiced," Jane said.

She then paused before going on. "After that, I ended up dropping out of the program. I moved to Milwaukee with a friend who also dropped out, and I found a job as a clerk with a wedding photographer."

"From public service to small business? How'd that work for you?"

"It was boring. I hated structure and routine. But I had to be practical. I went with the flow, trusting my ability to improvise. At least this job did not involve life-and-death situations. Probably divorce, based on statistics for the profession, but I didn't see that coming," she laughed.

"As soon as I learned the business, though, I suggested some improvements, and the owner implemented my suggestions. It made me happy. I felt like I was getting a college education in business without paying tuition. I would have gone back to college anyway and probably studied business once I'd saved enough.

"But then, my dad passed away. I had to move back home for a while, and my life came to a standstill. Eventually Mom sold the farm, and so I used my inheritance to finish my EMT certification."

"It seems like you moved away from the farm again for the last time."

"Yes, and this time, I went straight to a big city! While getting my EMT certificate, I took a minimum-wage job as a driver with a big ambulance service in St. Paul, Minnesota. Catching a pattern here?" Jane asked with a chuckle. "But there's a pattern in everything from the smallest blade of grass to the most distant planet. It's all about purpose and connection, and I was learning to respect that order."

Jane slowly pushed back from the desk to make just enough room to slip one leg over the other. "Strangely, though, as I was learning respect and order, I was recognizing how city life was out of sync. People seemed angry at each other and needed to prove in meaningless ways they were better than the guy next to them. I kept thinking about psychology classes and rats in a maze—everybody acted like they were the boss but most of them just worked for someone else. I knew then that I would determine my own fate or end up not being happy. At one point I thought, 'Maybe city people inhale too many gas fumes.' Ya know, most of the gas pumps are missing handle stoppers, so you need to squeeze them the whole time you fill up. That's a lot of fumes to breathe."

She paused to laugh at herself, and I could see the young girl she had described radiating from this accomplished, capable, and commanding female figure.

At that point, I couldn't hold out any longer and offered her a position on the team. I explained what to expect and suggested she consider working with one of the subcommittees that separately drove one of our four primary objectives. After discussing how to get her further information to her, we agreed to meet again soon.

Ten days passed before we got together again. Jane had emailed me about her interest in this subcommittee. It was called Executive Advisory Group Leadership Exchange, or EAGLE, a coaching-style development program for local companies. I knew by reading her email it spoke to her erudite reasoning.

We met for breakfast at eight-thirty near the state capitol, two hours before the first meeting of the full board. She took no time in shaping the goals into three action items. Before I had finished a second sip of my espresso, she handed me a packet with three folders that outlined a tactical approach to each of her initiatives.

"I didn't expect to be presented with homework so soon," I said, looking over my reading glasses.

She snapped closed her briefcase and asked, "Are you married with children?" We were back to her being in charge of the interview again, I thought. But before I could answer, she continued, "I'm asking because I told you I want to be a change maker, to leave this world a better place for my daughter, and I was wondering if you can relate?"

I unassumingly folded my hands over her packet. "One good interview leads to another, I suppose. Yes, I have been married for twenty-two years and have an amazing daughter. I'm motivated to be part of a financial justice solution in an economy that needs a reality check."

"Wow, me too! One daughter. She and I have a great relationship—at a time when so much seems to be negative, difficult, and even mysterious. I want to make social change for that wonderful girl and all young women like our daughters."

> **I want to make social change for that wonderful girl and all young women like our daughters.**

For the first time since we'd met, I saw Jane really relax, as if she was comfortable being her true self. Frankly, she did a good job in relaxing me, too.

"You said your creative outlet is dance," I casually said. "I have hobbies that include wildlife rescue, landscaping, and sailing. But for me, working on tasks such as this one is a creative outlet for me. Plus, I like getting to know people, and it's people like you who make the project fun. But without prying, I'd love to know more about your life—at whatever level you are comfortable with sharing."

For a moment, I wished I had kept my mouth shut. Did I ask for too much information?

"Sorry," I backpedaled. "I'm also a writer, and I enjoy people's stories."

Jane wasted no time in reassuring me. "I get political correctness, but we are all people, and some things go a bit too far—I'm an open book, pun intended!"

I smiled with relief and motioned "cheers" with her coffee cup. Then she continued her story.

"Perhaps it's my blonde hair. Men have always shown me a good share of attention. But my good relationships with my dad and brother kept me from making too many mistakes—until I met Clarence. He swept me off my feet. He was ten years older than I and a former county sheriff. He was working at a gravel company when I met him by chance in a convenience store in St. Paul. I was on my way home from driving the ambulance and still in my uniform shirt. He noticed my nametag, and I noticed his blue eyes. Enough said!"

> My good relationship with my dad and brother kept me from making too many mistakes—until I met Clarence. He swept me off my feet.

"If you're not comfortable, we can move on to something else," I said, still overly sensitive to our professional situation.

She didn't hesitate. "We only dated for two months before he asked me to marry him. My mistake?" She pounded her cup on the table. "He promised I'd have happiness with him for life, and

I believed it. Eleven months after saying 'I do,' I became pregnant with a baby girl, and by then I had a lot more knowledge about Clarence. He'd been abused as a child, and once the infatuation with me wore off, I became his victim. I didn't know what to do. So, I stuck it out and made a secret plan with the help of my brother."

I watched pensively as her hands gripped tighter around her coffee cup. "What did you do?"

"Well, after Angela, my darling angel baby, was born and we were still at the hospital, I sent Clarence out to buy a car seat. My brother and a social worker friend worked behind the scenes to get my doctor to agree that Angela and I could be released immediately after Clarence was gone. My brother drove us to his place in Madison and kept us in his apartment while I regained my strength. The social worker found a family shelter for me to move into with the baby. I had absolutely nothing but the things I'd brought with me to the hospital. They helped me file for a protective order, a divorce, and then pointed me toward day care for Angela—and a job."

Jane's crystal blue eyes filled with tears, but before they could fall, she caught them with a napkin.

"I suppose this makes me seem pathetic. Well, I *was* pathetic at the time, but somehow I kept going. My brother found me an old beat-up car, paid for insurance and gas, and I got a job as a dispatcher at an ambulance company in Madison. The shelter had a nursery. It broke my heart every day to leave Angela there, but I was determined we'd have our own place as soon as possible."

Trying to disguise my emotions, I interrupted before my own tears could fall. "This is probably a good time to drink up," I said. "It's almost time for us to go to the meeting."

Jane stopped as quickly as she had begun, and it was back to business as usual—almost as if we were snapping out of a dream.

Eager to switch gears, I said, "Let's go. Email me after the meeting with your thoughts on the group."

Over the next four months, the council of twelve made a great deal of progress in their efforts to develop new directives that could assist in economic advancement.

The fifth meeting of the full group took place one afternoon for more than three hours. When it was over, my intention was to skip dinner and head back to the office to catch up. I was about to call my wife when Jane pulled me aside.

"Will you do me a favor and let me take you for a quick bite to eat before you leave? I have an idea on one of the projects I'm working on, and I want your opinion."

"Well…okay," I said hesitantly. "I was calling my wife to tell her my plans for the evening, but I can add this in as well." I shrugged my shoulders with a "what else can happen" look.

"Okay. I'll call my husband; you call your wife. At dinner, we can accomplish two things at once. You need to have something in your stomach to get you through this tedious day, especially if you're planning to go back to the office."

Cell phones in hand, we took ten paces apart and put our plans in place. We then walked across the street to a Japanese restaurant. Over teriyaki bowls and hot tea, Jane explained her idea about a workforce training system.

"The main reason I wanted to speak with you is because those who have the greatest need for training are single women raising young children, just like I was back in the day."

> **Those who have the greatest need for training are single women raising young children.**

This statement suddenly clued me in on why she had taken on additional work after having already done so much for our Private Enterprise Council.

"Reliving that experience for the positive?" I queried, not sure how to make my point.

"Kind of. Those were some of the worst days of my life." Jane turned quiet for a moment, then said, "What makes you such a good listener?"

"I'm a student of how emotional intelligence leads to decision-making processes that determine quality of life," I replied. "I've learned a lot, but behavioral economics is a never-ending science. I've always been curious about how others navigate personal challenges, how they create, develop, and bring new ideas into the world. I'm also interested in how they work with their fellow humans, learn lessons, and build wealth in order to enjoy leisure. Everyone does it differently."

"Wow, cool stuff. Most people care only about themselves."

For the first time I could see the injured bird inside this woman of power. I needed to reassure her, so I said, "We are only human yet we're capable of overcoming great adversity. Please, go on."

She inhaled like a yogini in training and asked, "Do you know how difficult it is to take care of a child as a single parent? I had a good life but wanted better for Angela. It was difficult to work full time and then come home to feed, bathe, read to, entertain, and love her—then do laundry, clean, buy groceries, and pay bills. I was in a new city, had no friends, and didn't want to overtax my brother and sister-in-law. So, I learned to spread myself as thin as possible—in a good way."

"What do you mean?"

"Well, I knew I needed help. Once I got out of the shelter, I figured out a way to get training to move up the job ladder. My goal was to become a supervisor. At home, I budgeted my salary to pay the teenage girl next door to keep an eye on Angela when I tended to chores. It was during those times while being alone that I realized my strength and let go of my anger."

> **It was during those times while being alone that I realized my strength and let go of my anger.**

As Jane spoke about facing her challenges, it occurred to me that time alone to stay in touch with herself was one of the most important things she'd done to become the woman of action among her peers in the task force.

"Most people don't take that kind of time alone," I said, remembering her comment about being introverted.

"What did I have to lose? The baby was in good care. Better for me to go off by myself than continue to play strong and hold in the feelings that needed to be untangled and to let go. I couldn't afford therapy. So, I read library books late at night about how to overcome obstacles and advance my career. I didn't get much sleep."

"I can tell it was all part of what propelled you into the remarkable woman you are today!"

Jane ignored my compliment and continued to speak with a sharp focus. "Once I became a supervisor at the ambulance company, I worked even harder. To top it off, a lot of the people I supervised were male and old enough to be my dad. They resented me.

"And to make things worse, the few females there acted out against me. I had to keep telling myself that I was in a supervisory position, not a popularity contest. To counter their opposition, I committed to keep improving myself. My sister-in-law helped me put together a professional wardrobe from second-hand stores and garage sales. I let my hair grow so I could wear it in a professional style. I came to work wearing a little makeup and perfume each day. I created my own network of people to help me nurture myself, to take care of my child, to support my household in daily stuff like car repairs and visits to the dentist. Let me tell you, it's all the little things added up that bring people down. Without the support system I had, I wouldn't be talking with you now."

> **Let me tell you, it's all the little things added up that bring people down.**

The transformation of cocoon to butterfly was happening before my eyes. It humbled me to remember how difficult some people's live are and that all people struggle. For the moment, time had stopped and my fatigue from the day disappeared as Jane continued, unabated.

"I was working hard enough to keep things stringing along at home. At work, the more they dissed me behind my back, the more I acted with grace. I listened to people, learned from them, encouraged them, and asked what they wanted to do to make their work environment better. I was determined to dance my way through the resistance in any way, shape, or form it required. That's why music is embedded in my brain—when I listen, I feel it, and I move."

From what Jane had told me about her dance performance as a young girl, her strategy didn't surprise me. If she had been with my company, I would have matched her with someone to provide knowledge and social capital to help her better navigate our corporate culture. It was obvious she grew well from her own strength, but I had wondered if she'd done it all on her own.

"Was there anyone at the company who appreciated you as much as I do now?" I asked, trying not to sound patronizing.

"Well, that's why I wanted to have dinner with you. The best thing that ever happened to me was that I found a mentor—someone who took interest in me as a person. Being a woman and moving up the ladder has never been easy. It's getting better, but new and better mentorship programs are needed. Not just for women but for anyone, or for any company wanting to move to the next level."

"I totally agree."

"I'm glad to hear that, Kevin, because I want to work that into my committee."

Jane leaned in as if she had a secret message to reveal. "I'm telling you, job training is important, but it's the *personal support from an individual* that's the key to improving productivity. I need to know if you're on board with me on this one. What I plan to propose is that community colleges work along with my committee's workforce group to implement unique, personalized training programs. It will have some cost, but I can show the governor greater value. I've lived it and know it works."

I was taken aback by her honestly and intense emotion. On the spot, I knew we had to do even more than she had suggested.

> **On the spot, I knew we had to do even more than she had suggested.**

Not having a clue about the details of her plan, I was already sold. Then Jane gave me the second barrel. "Let me tell you exactly what happened to me," she continued. "For my review, after my second year on the job, my boss asked me to have lunch with her. She was the only woman executive the company had ever had. She offered to mentor me so I could develop skills that would keep advancing not only the company but our gender."

"Awesome!" I said. "I believe a strong mentorship sets up a symbiotic relationship between participants because you both learn. Do you think that's true?"

Shaking her head up and down like it was on a rubber band, she finally said, "Yes, and I embraced that opportunity. I took my mentor's advice often and learned valuable lessons. In fact, that mentorship is a big part of the reason I am who I am today."

It was no surprise that after Jane determined to crawl out of misfortune, a glowing career followed. To me, it was a telling example of listening closely to the sounds in the soul and not resting until something desirable manifested.

> **To me, it was a telling example of listening closely to the sounds in the soul and not resting until something desirable manifested.**

More curious than ever, I asked for the rest of the story. "So how does one jump yet another hurdle from being a single mom to owning a company?"

"My mentor invited me to sit at the table she'd bought at a fundraiser for at-risk kids. A guy named Neil sat at the same table. We started talking and just never stopped. We've been married for sixteen years now, and he has adopted Angela. At that time, he was the head of IT for the company that supplied our specialty equipment parts in charge of everything east of the Mississippi River. He's so smart."

Jane beamed like a high school cheerleader on her first date. There was no doubt she was still in love. But before I could utter a word, she went back in her fantasy, recalling the first days of her love.

"Soon after we were married, his company was bought by a national firm. Eventually, he was given an option to take a lump-sum severance package. He wanted out of the job anyway and always dreamed of owning his own company. We talked about it every day until we finally said, 'Let's do it!'"

Jane's enthusiasm ignited me as she spoke about the momentum that made her take steps like a graceful dancer to make their dream come true. I could see that her true joy came from opening her life with spiritual symmetry.

"To make this story short," she said slightly embarrassed, "Neil and I invested a small amount of money and a lot of sweat equity into an ambulance service. Our equity position was based on our ability and commitment to successfully expand the company and grow our market share in the Southwest.

"There wasn't much competition at the time, and we took small steps until things slowly fell into place. Our tremendous love as a couple and the need to bring others along for the fun kept us from too many pitfalls. We quickly adapted our abilities to lead the company through uncharted waters."

> **We quickly adapted our abilities to lead the company through uncharted waters.**

Her business acumen was spot on, just as I expected. And so was her connection to the world around her. "Good business owners often use multiple responses to adversity, and you were no different," I added.

"Yes, we analyzed separate pieces of the equation, managed debt, and used the cash flow we had available to make more money."

Her response was what I'd hoped for. But all of a sudden, a cloud of silence pervaded our space as if covering her in a kind of darkness I hadn't yet seen.

"You're always testing conclusions and re-executing solutions accordingly, right?" I asked.

She didn't answer.

"Are you alright?" I asked with concern.

She nodded. "Precisely. I used every opportunity to choose the right people to share the burden and distribute it over many shoulders."

"No," I stopped her and asked again, "Are you really all right? That's a personal question—you have already impressed me with your ability, so take a breath. It's been a long day for both of us. How are you holding up?"

She smiled shyly. "The treasures of life finally came to me, but it was a constant struggle."

"Yes," I nodded.

Then Jane looked at her untouched food as she continued. "Things got so bad after we started the business that one day, sitting in tears at a stoplight, I felt like I could go no further. Cash flow was tight, and I wasn't sure we could make payroll that month. My whole life rushed before my eyes, as if it were about to come to an end. Then I remembered my early days of sacrificing, saving, and stretching whenever I could, no matter how uncomfortable it felt," she said.

> **Then I remembered my early days of sacrificing, saving, and stretching whenever I could, no matter how uncomfortable it felt.**

"Yes, maybe things were bad. But after all I'd been through—the tears, laughter, and defeats—it became abundantly clear: *I will have the final word in how my destiny will be lived.*

"Then the blaring horns of impatient drivers behind me brought me back to the present. I drove through a light turned green ready to face seemingly insurmountable challenges. Pressing evenly on the accelerator, I moved confidently forward knowing that by applying my lifetime of stepping-stones, I would find a way!"

Before my eyes, a happy freckle-faced girl of eight who had no idea she'd one day confront a tragedy transformed herself into an amazing woman. After periods of deep self-doubt, this woman had picked up the shattered pieces of her complex life and found true success.

> **After periods of deep self-doubt, this woman had picked up the shattered pieces of her complex life and found true success.**

Being mesmerized by the power and inner beauty of this CEO, I had hardly touched my food. Knowing about her ability to manage events, balance her family life, and validate her emotional intelligence left me speechless—almost.

"A long road indeed," I said, pushing away the once-hot plate. "You learned as a child that if you can believe something in your mind and endure, then you can achieve. Most people fail that test, or should I say miss that point."

"Now, Kevin, you can understand why the giving-back-to-the-community program is so important to me."

"Yes, I can, Jane. And I can better understand how you lead by example and that you love helping others. There are no other surprises, right?" You have a good business, loving family, and an enjoyment of dancing …"

"I see where you're going here, Kevin!" as she interrupted me with the same tenacity, she showed the day she first entered my office. Jane had the floor, and I was glued to my chair yet again.

"The biggest payoff is the fact that I've reached a point of giving back to others because I was supported by my small community during a desperate time in my life. So today, Neil and I are instrumental in sustaining Helping Hands for Single Moms as our way of giving back."

I felt as if she lifted a jet off a runway. She began explaining about her group of businesswomen who support single moms to achieve career goals while rearing their children. "These moms have to go to college for training, certifications, or degrees so they can support their children better. We raise the money for their scholarships."

"The best part is we also help them when they face small emergencies such as a flat tire, a broken stroller, or various household problems so they can focus their time on nurturing their children. And once a month, the organization takes the families it supports to a park for the kids to play while the moms share ideas. I can help these moms because I know what they're going through."

> ## I can help these moms because I know what they're going through.

"That's very pragmatic and an intuitive use of your experience, Jane."

I knew now I was being prospected by this talented, ambitious figure before me, and I needed to pull my own weight. Besides, one good turn deserves another.

"Will you let me know when your next fundraiser is?" I asked. "I'd like to support it in your honor and to thank you for all the time you spent to help me achieve some of my goals."

"Sure, and thank you! When this Private Enterprise Council has done its work on this dance floor, I'll see you and your wife on the dance floor at our fundraisers."

With that, she smiled broadly, placed her napkin on the table, and concluded our talk for the evening.

Jane understood me as well as I understood her, and she had made a good bet that I'd help. About a year later, almost to that night of our last dinner together, the directives from the Council's economic development team were transitioned into government hands. As promised, it didn't take me long to make a handsome contribution to Jane's charity.

Once I had more time on my hands, I often thought about Jane like a spell of perfect weather. She had made a chaotic time more tolerable, and for that I was grateful.

One day out of the blue came an email inviting me to the installation dinner for the new president of Helping Hands, Jane's favorite charity for single moms. My first thought was to mail a check, but I decided (to my wife's dismay) to brush off the old tuxedo and attend. The dinner was on a weekend night, which was sacred family time at our house. But my wife and I made the effort to go to this red-carpet event on the designated evening. There, we saw a great deal of fanfare to impress all the high-rolling donors. About them, I whispered to my wife, "…they probably never got their hands dirty mucking stalls as Jane once did …"

I looked around the room, but Jane was nowhere to be found. We located our place at a table among cordial and polite people drinking plenty of wine. When the social formalities were done, I picked up the program to read the upcoming agenda. That's when I learned the incoming president being installed was my friend Jane. We were ecstatic!

The events of the night rolled on, and I waited with bated breath for the denouement. Finally, Jane walked on the stage to a thunderous applause. Her acceptance speech was humble, charming, and so much like the woman I had come to admire and respect.

> ## Her acceptance speech was humble, charming, and so much like the woman I had come to admire and respect.

My heart was filled with joy to see the crowd galvanized as she ended with an anecdote. Jane talked about a young girl on a farm who was shoveling cow manure from the barn floor into the gutters below, then slipped, fell down in the stall, and landed right in the muck.

People in the audience assumed this was about a disadvantaged client of Helping Hands. But after telling her mesmerizing story, Jane said, "That day marked the first time the young girl experienced hardship and learned to accept and overcome it. She felt no embarrassment. She simply climbed back up, cleaned herself off, held back a few tears, and started again. Shame might have overcome her if she'd allowed it, but she didn't."

Then she finished by saying, "When her dad learned about the incident, he gently poked fun about her getting a few more freckles. She felt no defeat, no sense of humiliation, no judgment about her slip-up. Her hardwired self-determination took hold that day, and she resolved to get right back to work—no worse for the setback."

At that point, Jane bowed her head slightly and the listeners leapt to their feet with applause. My heart was already in my chest and tears in my eyes. I knew from the start of the story the young girl was Jane herself.

> ## I knew from the start of the story the young girl was Jane herself.

It was she who overcame hard times and went on to achieve both personal and financial independence through courage and a delicate balance of strengths and weaknesses. She had learned to honor her true self.

Today, Jane's reward is a successful business and fulfillment as a mother, wife, and community leader. She derives pleasure from the beauty around her, both materially and spiritually. More than that, she has never lost sight of her struggles.

Although Jane's skills had vastly increased over time, one of her most important lessons—giving back—has remained a primary part of her success. With the talent of a maestro conductor, she has made all the moving parts of life work together for her benefit as she danced to the sound of the music in her heart.

You too can use Secret Success Standards from Jane's life story like the ones below as stepping-stones to your own accomplishments:

- Be willing to reach outside of your comfort zone to achieve the next level. It requires reframing situations to manage anxiety and fear by putting priorities in place.
- Never consider victimhood as an option, no matter what. Regard adversity as a challenge that manifests new options as you maintain focus, poise, and courage in daily living.
- Trust in the world around you in which everything has a purpose and a connection. Go with the flow. Listen to yourself and to what's around you. What you hear will guide you on your path.

CHAPTER 9

Of Humankind

I had to make my own living and my own opportunity.
But I made it! Don't sit down and wait for the opportunities to
come. Get up and make them.
–Madam C. J. Walker

A lonely childhood heightened by poverty and illness defined Brandon Bartholomew's early life.

When we first met, I had been focusing on environmental stewardship as well as child advocacy, helping kids in group homes who had suffered abuse and abandonment. The horse therapy program for renegade kids who were wild at heart, was working. Now, I had the opportunity to turn my desire to supporting at risk kids in a more financially direct way.

After exploring a financial literacy program, we decided at the last minute, to set up a small nonprofit. Funded by my company and other donors, we awarded seed-money grants to community organizations.

The day I met Brandon Bartholomew it was raining lightly. His grant request, *to improve the human condition,* won him an opportunity to present to our Board of Directors and he was waiting in the anteroom. I had no idea what to expect when this handsome, understated man entered the conference room.

* * *

Brandon Bartholomew was dressed in a dark-gray wool suit, white starched shirt, and purple tie, making it hard to tell he was a thin man. His tortoiseshell glasses accented the ebony color of his skin, eyes, and close-cropped graying hair. His demeanor was serious—until he smiled like a morning sunrise.

Not readily apparent from his façade was what he had overcome. As I later learned, Brandon's father had died when he was eight. His mother raised him on her nurse's salary, but she also died early in his life.

Brandon was fortunate to find activities such as science, academics, and business that bolstered his spirit. He'd preferred sports but grew to accept his limitations as an athlete. His back-up plan was to become highly educated and use his practical knowledge to adopt nontraditional alternatives.

The week following Brandon's presentation, the panel granted his request for funding, and he was informed by email. After the long Veterans Day weekend, I went in my office to catch up on a stack of unread mail that had arrived before the holiday. Among the credit-card offers, bills, and advertisements was a handwritten note on personal stationery from Brandon Reddox Bartholomew. "Thank you very much," he wrote, "for giving financial support to improve the way physicians serve impoverished patients in central Mississippi." He closed the letter with an invitation to visit him at his home in Starkville, Mississippi.

The letter struck me as unusual. Most responses of gratitude are staged and rather superfluous. They arrive on letterheads of the receiving entity, addressed collectively to the entire panel. Why had this man reached out with thanks in such a way?

Intrigued, I called the number on the enclosed business card thinking I'd have to leave a voicemail. On the second ring, though, Brandon picked up the phone.

"Hello, this is Brandon."

"I've just read the note you sent me and wanted to call and talk with you. Do you have time?" I said, trying to conceal my astonishment I'd actually reached him live.

"Of course I do!" he said in a soft titter. "My note was just a common courtesy."

"Well, it made me want to know you better," I said, smiling, as if he could see through the phone. "I wanted to thank you for the invitation to visit you in Mississippi."

He replied, "Once we get a few medical clinics outfitted the way I envision, you can take a tour. Kevin, you asked the most questions at my presentation. I assumed you'd either like to see the results on the generosity of your 501(c) as soon as possible, or you were actually stonewalling the project."

I was stunned, not by his openness but by the sound of his voice. It was so non-confrontational, I simply moved to my next thought without taking his comment personally.

"Thank you. Yes, I'd like to visit the project and want to stay in touch with the progress beforehand," I said.

> "I'd like to visit the project and want to stay in touch with the progress beforehand," I said.

"In your presentation, Brandon, you gave a lot of facts about the work, and I know you're backing this with some of your own money and money from another community group. But I'd like to know how you got involved with this work in the first place. You're from Mississippi. Did you grow up in the South?"

"Yes …"

Detecting a sigh, I said nothing. I didn't want him to feel uncomfortable. But I wanted an answer, so I patiently waited.

"I was born in rural Mississippi in a small town called Aberdeen, right when the civil rights protests were occurring. Mine is the kind of story most people would prefer to leave in the past where it belongs."

He paused, and I again remained silent.

"Basically, it included poverty, grief, discrimination, and loneliness. But I had a little bit of good fortune, too."

It was the first time I heard him truly laugh, but somehow the laugh seemed misplaced. The moment flew by, and he began again.

"Any human life can be touched by those things. What makes my story unique is how I dealt with it. And by the way, I know you're a collector of stories, Kevin."

Brandon had obviously done his homework.

"We don't know each other well," he continued, "and it's not easy for me to open up. I can talk about the project, but talking about myself—that's more difficult."

> I can talk about the project, but talking about myself—
> that's more difficult.

I felt I needed to respond equally. "It's true that I'm curious. But please share what works for you. Associations always have to start somewhere, and in my view, ours started with your note. There's something special about your gratitude, and I hope you will share your story with me. Thank you again for extending an invitation for me to come to town."

Recognizing I was right, Brandon cleared his throat. "As poor as we were when I was growing up, my mother taught me to be appreciative and hospitable. As for telling my story, I'd like to think on it. Maybe it's best if we stick to business in the meantime."

"I'd be honored if you decide to call me back. I'll let you go, but thank you very much for the note. Even if I don't hear from you, I will indeed visit once your clinics are up and running."

Late the next day, I was catching up with news online and a familiar number came up on my phone. I answered it.

"Hello, this is Brandon Bartholomew. We spoke yesterday. Are you still willing to listen to my life story? Because if you are, I've had a change of heart."

"A change of heart?"

"Well, yes I . . . I have. I didn't expect a response from my note because I often spend time taking actions that seem beneficial without expecting any sort of return. Most people are self-centered. I believe we should escape from our own orbits every now and then and reach out. When I told you I didn't want to share my life story, I was being self-centered. I then recognized you were reaching out to me.

"So, do you have time to talk for a while now?"

The stillness of the afternoon felt hollow all of a sudden. The man on the other end of the phone made me feel awkward, yet I was intrigued and forced an answer.

"Yes, of course I have time for you," I said, grabbing my freshly poured glass of scotch. As the ice cubes rattled, Brandon cleared his throat.

"It's not easy to reach back into childhood. I know it sounds cliché, but I wish I knew *then* what I know *now*," he started.

> I know it sounds cliché, but I wish I knew then what I know now.

"As an only child, my childhood was lonely, and I was sickly—I had asthma—and we were poor. My dad worked as a janitor at the plant where PVC plastic is made, but he died when I was eight, likely from work hazards. My mom worked at the Head Start preschool, and after Dad died, she studied to earn her vocational nurse certification. My parents paid a lot of attention to me until my father passed. After that, my mother was either in school or at work, and she left me mostly alone."

As Brandon spoke, I scrambled for pen and paper, nearly tipping my scotch. It was stunning to hear him spout like a fire hose about the kind of difficult life that, up until that point, I had only read about.

He continued, "My mother influenced my life. She had little education but a very caring spirit. It was because of her that I got help from several good doctors. That's what gave me an interest in the medical profession. I knew I had to do well in school if I wanted to be a doctor, and I got off to a good start, especially after discovering I liked chemistry. The public schools I attended in Aberdeen gave me a bare-bones education through high school. It wasn't until later in life that I learned how people from all places were benefitting from well-funded educations."

As the sun bounced off a copper vase in my study, I had a sense there was a good reason for me to be right here, right now.

"After my dad passed, I looked for and did any job I could get to help put food on our table," Brandon continued, barely taking a breath. "I can finally smile at the imagined me—coughing, sickly, thinking only about my schoolwork and being paid in small change to help neighbors with their gardens, garbage and other chores."

He finally took a breath—or so it seemed.

"Often, people just gave me cans of food in exchange for my work. I know my mom worked hard, and it satisfied me to ease her burden this way if only slightly. It was easier than feeling the oppression of the day. She set the example for me. She wanted me to have a better life."

> **My mother set the example for me. She wanted me to have a better life.**

"You had some strong motivation, Brandon," I said as I slipped off my shoes, ready to relax and hear more.

"Yes, I was blessed. My mother was the strongest, gentlest person I've ever known. It was difficult for me to make friends, and I know that wore down her heart.

"It wasn't an easy life, but there were rewards. When it came to school, I always scored well on tests. When I was a senior in high school, a teacher arranged for me to obtain scholarship money toward college tuition."

"You were fortunate to have a teacher who cared."

"It's true," he said. "I worked at various part-time jobs through college to pay the rest of my tuition."

"What was your undergraduate degree?"

"I studied chemistry, thinking I'd be a teacher. It didn't work out for me to teach, though—I was meant for the sanctity of a lab. When I finished my BS at Mississippi State, I wanted to go on with my studies, and I did. I was working part-time jobs and getting loans to pay tuition when I got into the master's program at Ole Miss. I had no time to focus on relationships outside of my jobs, my mom, and my studies."

Rubbing my toes together under my desk like I was sitting by a warm fire, I probed further.

"According to the information on the grant, you ended up in medical equipment sales."

"Yes. My mother had been sick while I was in college and died the month before I earned my master's degree in chemistry. Only two people came to see me graduate—a lady who used to hire me to help her clean her house and the high school teacher who believed in me."

I took a long sip of scotch with the perfect blend of melted ice, but the flavor couldn't quench my sadness for this still lonely man.

Brandon pushed on. "With my mom gone, I lost motivation. The kind of grief I felt is a disease unto itself. So, I packed up and left Mississippi for Texas, all alone."

"Texas?"

"A colleague of one of my professors introduced me to a retired medical researcher. After an extensive 'get-to-know-you' process, I was offered a chance to work as one of the assistants to Brian Johns, MD. Have you heard of him?"

"Sorry, no."

"An amazing man. His lab is at Baylor College of Medicine."

Brandon finally paused and then said, "I'll be right back—I need a glass of water."

I heard the phone drop onto a hard surface and thought about the difficulty of those life-changing decisions he had to make. When Brandon returned, I asked the usual financial question, "Had you paid off your student loans when you moved to Texas to switch careers?"

"Of course not," he laughed. "It took years to pay them off, but I was fortunate to get a job working with Dr. Brian Johns. He was almost a legend."

Brandon's answer came back more cavalier than I had expected, so I restructured my inquiry. "You made a clean break from your former life in Mississippi then, right?" Asking that question was like getting caught looking at his homework that he didn't let me finish.

He replied, "The opportunity felt right. I remember writing out my goals—which involved research on stem cells. I wanted to be one of those African Americans who could rise from a lineage of oppression and make a difference. I kept visualizing myself having a good job in a laboratory.

"But once I got inside the medical facility at the Baylor School of Medicine, I was overwhelmed by my own insignificance. At that moment, the obstacles in front of my dreams were intimidating. Then I met Dr. Johns."

> **At that moment, the obstacles in front of my dreams were intimidating. Then I met Dr. Johns.**

"What was so special about him?" I asked.

As Brandon went on about Dr. Johns and his research, I began connecting the dots and the light bulb finally went on.

"Wait, I think I heard that name when I was on the board of a biotech startup," I said, slightly panicked about my age-related memory.

"We were pitching venture-capital companies without much luck. One of my colleagues had known Dr. Johns, and he suggested we sign him on as a medical advisor to increase our funding chances. If it's the same guy, he was a force of nature!"

Though it brought up the bittersweet memory of my prior business model gone south, I affirmed, "So, he was the doc who gave you the opportunity to get your feet wet in the industry."

"Without a doubt," Brandon said. "I remember waiting by the admitting desk the first time I met him. The chaos in the waiting area suddenly quieted as a long thin figure glided to the desk. The waiting room appeared to shrink in contrast to the larger-than-life doctor who stood at its center. It was Dr. Brian Johns, cowboy handsome and movie-star elegant. Even the receptionist blushed!"

After an awkward moment of silence, I said, "If I remember correctly, Dr. Johns' physical strength seemed to equal his intellect, and his work ethic was unparalleled. Although his ego was as big as his reputation, he used both wisely to attract the attention he wanted."

"Well, Dr. Johns' nickname was Rocket—a testament to the momentum he carried. His ego was built on character and fortified by dignity. From the moment we met, I felt a kinship or maybe a fascination with him. It was like nothing I'd ever felt. And I wanted to be like him. He was always first to arrive in the clinic and last to leave. He expected nothing but excellence from his research and from the people around him. I thrived in that environment."

> **Dr. Johns expected nothing but excellence from his research and from the people around him. I thrived in that environment.**

I recalled the nickname Rocket but not the doctor's charm.

"We shared a similar determination to improve the human condition for the betterment of mankind," Brandon summarized with adoration.

"I, too, share that, Brandon," I said. "And I'm familiar with the kind of intelligent risk-taking Dr. Johns practiced. But it appeared to me a lot of ego made up his molecular compound."

It seemed Brandon found this comment neither entertaining nor witty. He replied, "Dr. Johns was an excellent boss as well as a friend. I worked hard in his lab and indeed matched his long hours and intensity."

With a slight sigh, he continued, "I was never sure I could rise to his level. If I remained an assistant in the shadow of his greatness, I could be well compensated, but doing that would have compromised my own calling. It got down to measuring cause and effect—and realizing only certain parts of a person can successfully fit in one place. That's when I made the difficult decision to leave Dr. Johns and look for a job outside the lab."

In his grant request, Brandon stated he had gone from scientist to the business of medical-equipment sales. It seemed like a stretch given his propensity for shyness and love of research, so I was curious to know more about his decision.

By now, it had gotten dark. Cassidy, our dog, found his way next to my chair. I was hoping my wife would be along soon to let him out. Because opportunities rarely come when you are ready, I ignored Cassidy and pursued this conversation.

"You seem to be driven by the practical knowledge of science. What made you decide to investigate the chemistry of commerce?" I asked.

Unfazed by repartee, Brandon continued in a dead-pan tone. "I recognized that the kind of work Dr. Johns was doing required shipments of newer and better equipment, so I spoke with a medical supply company used by the university. This led me to leaving Baylor to increase my exposure to the world and learn more about how to do business within the realm of medical science.

"I presented a plan to the executives of the Houston-based company that supplied lab equipment. They were eager to hire a new sales rep like me who had insight into the workings of a biochemical research lab and could identify the need for the company's more advanced products. It was a great move that taught me a lot about industry and business."

Perhaps the light from the small desk lamp surrounded by the darkness of the whole house made me realize what a beacon this man had become.

> Perhaps the light from the small desk lamp surrounded by the darkness of the whole house made me realize what a beacon this man had become.

It became obvious that he gathered information and made quick associations to understand new concepts. From there, he applied them in useful ways. Yet at the same time, he combined his spiritual self with his warm personality.

"Fascinating," I said. "What did this move do to your friendship with Dr. Johns?"

"We remained friends, and our paths continued to cross. There were many expensive dinners paid for by the medical-equipment firm. Sometimes those nights ran late. Once we were even asked to leave a restaurant because the manager wanted to close. We ended up walking shoulder to shoulder through the River Oaks, Tall Timbers section of Houston like two schoolboys, passing a bottle of Frapin Cuvee 1888 between us.

"Those were fun days, but soon after that, my role at the company changed." He paused for a moment.

"When I moved to the international side of the business and began traveling the world, I saw less and less of Dr. Johns. The last time was in the hospital before he died …" Brandon's voice trailed off, and I sensed he was still grieving.

"Yes," I said as gently as possible. "I remembered hearing a rumor that Dr. Johns suffered complications from AIDS, but that was never confirmed. I'm sorry—it must have been difficult for you to lose his friendship."

"As tough as the deaths of my mother and father were, in some ways his death was even more difficult," Brandon said apprehensively. "I miss him and still think about him often."

I listened for a hint of where the conversation would go next and then said, "Let's talk about your efforts to get these clinics built and running efficiently as written in the grant request."

Brandon breathed a sigh of relief for the change of conversation and enthusiastically replied, "To get to that, let me give you some history about the business of lab-equipment sales and how I was able to understand the cycle of economic gain.

"When oil prices increased causing an upward cost pressure on core capital goods like lab equipment, I was urged to increase revenues by building a sales team."

"Your life went from test tubes to sales guru?" I asked.

"You can say that. It's an irregular course, but it's exactly what happened. I was a decent salesman, but I was better at selecting and screening the people who could really sell. That's what brought the financial rewards."

"It must have had something to do with the way you approached science, except it paid more," I chuckled, hoping I'd get a laugh back.

"Absolutely," he said sternly. "I made a good living in the lab and did even better with the medical-equipment company. I invested in both pension plans and practiced personal thriftiness. Growing up with very little taught me I didn't need much. Then one day, I realized I was actually financially secure for the first time in my life!"

> **Then one day, I realized I was actually financially secure for the first time in my life!**

Brandon took a deep, but tired, breath. "That also was the day I asked myself what I wanted next and found that my heart still desired more. I'd always hoped my interest in education and the help I'd been given by doctors and nurses when I was young would lead to service in the health care industry."

"So, what was the tipping point that moved you to change to health care accessibility in the South?" I asked, wondering how a naturally timid man could make such a key paradigm shift.

"Well, let me see," he said, breathing more evenly. "I had finished a successful European sales trip and was asked to stop over and visit a group of doctors on Long Island. They were on the fence about purchasing high-priced imaging equipment. I worked up my pitch while in flight, but I wasn't prepared to see what I witnessed when I arrived in the waiting room.

"It was late afternoon and the room looked like the Department of Motor Vehicles with almost every seat taken. As I moved through the mass of humanity, I noticed the teary eyes of an elderly woman. When I asked if she was okay, she told me she'd been waiting over an hour for her orthopedic surgeon to check her recent hip operation. She told me she was all alone in the world— aside from her husband of sixty years, who couldn't hear.

"Before I could say anything, the admitting nurse announced that one of the doctors in the medical group was not expected in the office for another thirty minutes. A palpable wave of discomfort washed through the waiting room followed by questioning glances from person to person. As her tears welled up again, she got called to see her doctor, so I volunteered to help her to the exam room."

> As her tears welled up again, she was called to see her doctor, so I volunteered to help her to the exam room.

Brandon was painting the scene well. "We waited another twenty minutes in the exam room while I tried to comfort her. Finally, the door flew open and the physician slapped an X-ray on the light board like he was practicing a golf swing. Without making eye contact with his patient, he barked, 'How do you feel?' as he admired the X-ray of his handiwork. The woman softly asked how long it would be before she could walk on her own again, knowing the answer meant the difference between her personal freedom or her dependence on others.

"'You may never walk again without a cane,' the doctor said without emotion. 'Your hip may never fully heal.' With no further explanation, he told her he had done a good repair job, and she should see him again in thirty days. Then he disappeared as quickly as he'd entered."

I had a sense Brandon was holding back tears. He continued, "I helped the woman back to the reception area, where her sobs broke the morbid silence."

Now unable to find words, Brandon hesitated. I understood from my own experiences how jet-lagged and bleary-eyed he must have been that day. Recalling his comments about childhood and the deaths of his parents in an ill-equipped hospital, I knew he felt distraught.

Then he continued, "At that point, I felt that medicine was broken and knew I wanted to do something about it. I just didn't know what to do yet."

> **I felt that medicine was broken and knew I wanted to do something about it. I just didn't know what to do yet.**

Brandon took another large breath. "The income gap between the doctors and the people suffering indignities in the waiting room was so graphic, I couldn't accept people being victimized by the special interest groups in their health care."

"I assume at that point you didn't care to close the imaging equipment deal," I stated.

"No. Because I was so angry, I knew there was no chance of even coming close. I grabbed a cab ride back to the airport and put myself through some paces during the ride. Then, as I sat hoping for a standby seat to Houston, I remembered the people who were kind to me when I was poor, lonely, and sick. I felt that all of them were motivated by a purpose greater than money."

"Sounds like your philosophy about money changed that day," I said, glad to hear him embrace my own beliefs.

"Yes. You know, in my youth, I wondered what life would be like if I had money, but I mostly wanted someone to share my goals and dreams. I always shied away from intimacy and tended to avoid social settings. I spent most of my time inside my own mind and, except for Dr. Johns, I had few friends.

"But when I walked out of that office on Long Island, I knew something inside had changed. I was ready to join a fight for *dignified, effective health care for all* at a local level. It still keeps me up at night because I know it affects the well-being of thousands of people in rural places like where I lived as a child."

> **It still keeps me up at night because I know it affects the well-being of thousands of people in rural places like where I lived as a child.**

In that split second, I was certain that awarding the grant to Brandon had been the right decision. I felt delighted, and apparently so did my dog. His ears perked up at the sound of my wife coming in the door. He knew he'd soon be fed.

Excited by the same prospect, I said, "Seems we've come full circle in this conversation, my friend. We're back at the reason why your grant application was so astutely approved. You made my day! Thank you so much for the time today."

On that note, we agreed to keep in touch, and our conversation ended. I had promised to visit one of his clinics after it was revamped to serve—with dignity—patients like the elderly woman Brandon met in New York.

As time went on, I followed the progress of this compassionate man with a keen interest in his journey to improve the lives of others. I became eager to visit.

A few months went by without any communication between us. Then one morning I read an article about Brandon Bartholomew; he'd been interviewed for a business blog that profiled people doing cutting-edge work in health care. Brandon's profile showed foresight into how health practices could benefit economics and lifestyles within small towns.

It seemed Brandon found a connection of spirit and mind that gave him the power to overcome childhood disadvantage and attain his goals. He consolidated insights into patterns that would change what was wrong. Having no patience for pettiness and inefficiency, he used his training as a starting point and approached his new goal with a concentrated effort.

In his interview, Brandon said he'd explored target markets and profiled primary care providers to determine areas with the most acute need for reform. Then he put together a team of associates to collect facts and reveal the true needs of the business practice and the community. After a short time, he'd received enough needs-specific information to construct a tailored business model that would satisfy those needs.

Glancing up from reading, I noticed I was holding my coffee cup in midair. Not only had I not put it down, but it was empty—as empty as my stomach. I could hear the sounds of breakfast being made and soon the wholesome smells followed. But I had a need to read further.

The article said the markets Brandon selected were in rural Mississippi where more than half a million people could benefit from the improved health care structure he'd proposed. Doctors in these underpopulated areas had complained about the unwillingness of the people to seek medical care. It wasn't unusual for young doctors to close up their practices and move to more lucrative communities.

> **It wasn't unusual for young doctors to close their practices and move to more lucrative communities.**

I couldn't help myself. I picked up the phone.

"Wow, Brandon, I just read the article you sent from the medical magazine. I know we are not scheduled to talk for another month, but I wanted to hear more about this."

"Any time, Kevin." He said this with more confidence in his voice than ever before and wasted little time with pleasantries.

"In addition to the grant money your board gave me, I got a call from the dean of the medical school at University of Mississippi. I had sent him a business plan with my scientific support, and he was ready to sponsor part of the project by sending doctors, nurses, pharmacists, and other health practitioners with newly minted degrees to the clinics."

"Congratulations. That's outstanding!" I said. "It all seems to be coming together."

"In addition to staffing, we got some funding from the university to keep innovating," he said in the tone of a peer.

Brandon went on about his days of arduous discussions and accepting funding from the university's foundation in exchange for a minority equity position in the company. He described how the medical school would benefit from increased recognition, patient care research, and service to the community.

I listened to this scientist-turned-businessman—a man who was reluctant to even speak to me at all in the beginning. I was captivated by how Brandon used big-picture insight to synthesize facts into solid plans to implement his vision.

"Slow down, my friend. My wife Gretchen is cooking breakfast, and unless you want to be the cause of a man gone homeless, I need to get to the kitchen."

We both laughed out loud and hit "End" simultaneously.

As I walked down the hall, my sense of pride and accomplishment was laced with excitement, not about the feast that awaited me but knowing that, in the months to come, I would witness a miraculous transformation. It was happening not only in medical care in the south but in a man who was a child during the south's most shameful atrocity in history.

The next day, I got up bright and early, my espresso cup back in hand. This time it was full, and the black hot liquid quivered as I watched the clock for a reasonable time to call Brandon. Finally, I hit speed dial.

"Hello, Brandon, I hope it's not too early to call."

"Oh heavens no. I've been working since six in the morning," he replied.

"You know I'm a procedures and protocols guy, and I'm eager to hear about the secrets to your success.

Brandon let out an uncharacteristically loud laugh.

"It was simple. We set up our prototype office and took steps to find other doctors who wished to improve how they ran their medical practices and the service their patients received. Then I sent consultants—salespeople like me—to help them set goals, implement systems, and increase revenue. Once they signed a contract for ongoing consulting services, our team began indoctrinating them in the well-developed and easy-to- understand methods for practice management."

This time I was ready. "Brandon, I want to record some of our conversation for our board. Do you agree?

"Of course; it's the least I can do." And with another rowdy laugh he went on like he hadn't stopped.

"Specifically, we sent operation teams to install new phone systems designed to distribute incoming calls by category to action centers either within the office or at specialized locations in the corporate headquarters. These systems also sent patients automatic reminders to schedule follow-up appointments and annual physicals. This alone generated increased visits within the first month.

"Next, tenant-improvement specialists reconfigured the front office. Staff members were cross-trained. Before long, hourly productivity usually increased, and the marginal administrative staff was reduced. This allowed for the hiring of more practitioners who helped boost profit margins. Having more nurses, physician's assistants, and other health care professionals boosted the office's capacity."

> Having more nurses, physician's assistants, and other health care professionals boosted the office's capacity.

Knowing a leveraged medical practice would speak well to our board members, I wrote time-segment notes of the recording to serve as my refence points. I also paid close attention to inflections in his voice.

"Once the underlying support staff was in place," Brandon continued as if he were speaking to a crowd, "my consultants finally focused on the physicians. With the greatest ability to affect per-hour revenue, the goal was for doctors to maximize their bottom line by seeing more patients.

"Technology systems were modified so the billing, recordkeeping, and compliance issues required only minimal physician involvement. That meant they could focus their time on patients. Also, kiosks were set up in waiting rooms so patients could log in to complete details of their charts and update their insurance information.

"We structurally upgraded reception areas and exam-room configurations so patients could move through the intake and exam process with ease. And we revamped insurance protocols so the physicians themselves were no longer required to deal with insurance except to ensure regulatory accuracy."

Brandon continued to speak as I scribbled notes about the minutes and seconds from the recorder.

"In addition, we implemented a system to periodically evaluate insurance carriers for best practices."

"Amazing!" I said with an extra syllable.

"Why y-yes I am," Brandon said mocking me. "These formulas proved to be a boon for business. Offices now run with the metered consistency of a heartbeat. Face time with patients has increased along with practice revenues, and thus the quality of life for both doctors and patients has improved. My dream of offering improved health care in the rural South is being fulfilled."

Then without taking a pause, he asked the question I was waiting for. "So when do you want to come visit? It's time."

This marked not only an investment success but also the unleashing of a power in a man who would do good on many levels.

"I'm free at the end of the month if you are, but I have something else to add," I said touting my own experience. "It's rare for someone to transition from science to business, but you blended the two into a winning combination."

Brandon was suddenly as quiet as he'd been during our first phone call. In fact, I thought the call had accidentally dropped. Then I could hear a smile in Brandon's voice as he replied, "Two things keep repeating themselves in my life. One is the challenge and sheer satisfaction of doing the right thing, and the other is the challenge of completing my commitment to others."

> Two things keep repeating themselves in my life. One is the challenge and sheer satisfaction of doing the right thing, and the other is the challenge of completing my commitment to others.

As a scientist, he knew that just as hydrogen and oxygen react in a chemical event, so too could behavioral elements react to allow doctors and patients to make their dreams come true.

"Thank you," I said.

"And thank you, Kevin, for believing in me.

After we hung up, I sat in thought about Brandon whose life embodied the analysis of options and the realization that there were no perfect solutions. As a scientist, he counted on engagement and perseverance to invent new paths of exploration. The very nature of this exploration led him to walk on the edge of a brave new world that has opened doors to treatments or cures.

Success in science and business can sometimes prove elusive, but Brandon explored options that led to advanced achievement for medical care and himself.

Worn down by modern society, many people surrender when they've had enough, but Brandon Bartholomew did not. He always challenged himself, and it kept building his character.

You too can use Secret Success Standards from Brandon's life story like the ones below as stepping-stones to your own accomplishments:

- Work hard to honor each opportunity that comes your way. Write down goals that will challenge you and require growth.
- Make a difference in the lives of others. Over the years, Brandon used medical science to improve the human condition for those who suffered. It transformed his life and made him millions.
- Analyze options and realize there are no perfect solutions. Over time, Brandon varied his goals to find professional satisfaction.

CHAPTER 10

Fire and Water

Stop by the 19th hole and have a couple of aces without a slice. But stop before you see bogey men or get trapped. And if you happen to be balancing your checkbook, remember to replace the divots.
—Art Cashin

You can learn a lot in eighteen holes of golf. Although I must admit, hitting a small ball with a stick was never the lesson. I used balls in sports—mostly baseballs—and I liked sticks—mostly to *stick check* opposing players in lacrosse. Standing on a wide flat stick to slide down waves crashing behind me, was ultimately better then chasing a ball with one.

Don't get me wrong; being in the joys of nature and the smell of freshly cut grass kept me playing golf. Perhaps my only hesitation was "keeping my head down" because it distracted me from the beautiful open space. But the overriding reason I played golf was to enjoy time with friends and gain insights into lives of intriguing people I hadn't met.

Looking back, most people in any foursome had unique and unusual stories. The most unexpected though, was a couple I saw regularly giving a friendly wave in my neighborhood. I had no idea how interesting they actually were until one day, their intricate and private world opened right before me like a long rolling fairway.

* * *

It was parent night for our daughter Rachel's back-to-school orientation when we bumped into my wife's friend, who was co-chairing the fall fundraiser with her. The women hugged and then their husband introductions happened. While the wives caught up, I had a dutiful conversation with Philip, Eva's husband, about business, sports, and how weary we'd become listening to the principal, who seemed intent on running for superintendent.

Once my wife Gretchen and I were across the parking lot, I simply asked about the couple as a frame of reference. She excitedly obliged for the entire ride home.

Materially speaking, Eva had been raised with nothing while Philip had too much. Together, through honest self-examination, they developed their best traits and integrated them into a package of shared power. Their self-discipline and rational approach to finance allowed frugality to be an advantage, which created substantial net worth for them.

> **Their self-discipline and rational approach to finance, allowed frugality to be an advantage, which created substantial net worth.**

Since Gretchen and Eva would be closely working together, we decided to get better acquainted with this couple. But it wasn't until months later that we planned to play golf together.

I called the pro shop early in the week to be sure to get a tee time. On the day before we planned to play, there was no need to ask questions about the couple with whom we were to play. The moment I walked through the door, my wife proceeded to tell me all she knew up to that point about Philip and Eva.

My history lesson began during wine in our yard with my wife barely stopping to take a sip. Thanks to subtle shadows on the golf course from a lazy setting sun, I felt relaxed and focused on listening.

"Eva got through college on a work-study program," Gretchen mused, wine glass in hand. "She met Philip in the dining hall where she worked wiping tables and mopping floors. The fact that he even talked with her was fantastic," she quipped. "Because his family's wealth was well known."

"But Eva's beautiful," I defended, understanding why any man would talk to her.

"Yet they were such opposites," she countered.

"But beauty attracts," I returned.

"And opposites attract—perhaps more so than beauty," she corrected.

Having been put in my place, Gretchen went on. "They each came from dysfunctional families, and that's what they have in common."

She then paused with passive loathing and said, "I know you don't care, but I'm sure you're wondering how Philip maintained his financial success during the economic downturn."

"Yes I was, darling. You're right as usual."

"Well, if you can withhold the hilarious comments, I'll tell you more after dinner."

Our family dog had a way of letting us know when tensions were too high or if it was time to eat. Fortunately, there was always more food than tension, and that night when I looked up, he had his nose pinned to the door. Being well trained, we followed suit and went inside the house to prepare dinner. Indoors, our conversation centered on details of my wife's upcoming golf event and was sprinkled with anecdotes about our daughter.

After dessert, we went outside to sit by the fire and watch the stars. In this completely relaxed mood, the topic of Philip and Eva came up again. My wife explained how Eva navigated through her low-income upbringing and how it was love at first sight when she met Philip.

"Eva has been a great help to me," Gretchen said with a blue-blooded sigh. "She has great work ethic, good perspective, and knows a little about everything—from untangling skirmishes between parent volunteers to how the after-school snack bar can make more money.

"We played nine holes together one morning last week. She's such a good new golfer—almost as good as me and I've been playing since I was ten."

"How's Philip's game?" I asked.

"Probably pretty good. His grandparents sold some of their land to a golf course developer in the early 1900s. He grew up on an estate and probably learned golf at a very early age."

"He's never worked a day in his life, right?" I said, passive-aggressively defending my average, not stellar, golf handicap.

"Philip was a business major when he met Eva and went on for an MBA. He came from wealth, but his family situation was, well, maybe he'll tell you the details. I think he started a company right after he earned that MBA. You two could likely find a lot to talk about. But be careful not to be so fixated on his story that you lose focus on your swing. I don't want to hear you yelling 'Fore!' all day."

Knowing what was coming next, I deferred responding and, instead, thought about Philip and Eva's situation. The charity fundraiser ironically happened during a time the American Dream was headed for a fall. Stock markets were plunging and so were home prices, the primary assets of most American families. I recalled that night at the school that after I mentioned my midrange mergers-and-acquisitions experience, Philip said something about recapitalization.

This recollection made me wonder even more about how Philip and Eva had managed to make their economic dream come true and stay afloat during these unprecedented economic times. I planned to find out as politely as possible the next day on the links.

On Saturday morning, the four of us met in the pro shop at our country club. After pleasantries, my wife and Eva told us they wanted to spend time together talking shop, so I shared a cart with Philip.

As we pulled off to the first tee box, I teed off the conversation. "My wife Gretchen mentioned that you're in the transportation business. Planes, trains, and automobiles?" I asked while opening a sleeve of balls.

Philip laughed loud enough so even our wives, who were well behind us, could hear. "Started with food carts for street vendors, moved into golf carts, and now we distribute any vehicle that you don't need a license to drive. I'm kind of an accidental entrepreneur."

"Accidental? That's how I play golf, but I'm here for the fun and always curious about a good success story."

"Sounds like a perfect day!" Philip said in a pleasant tone.

The day was textbook, moderate temperatures, and just enough wind to keep a breeze on our faces and a ball straight and long down the fairway.

"Well," Philip said as we pulled up to the first tee box, "when I finished my MBA, I got a job with a transportation company and worked my way up. It was about the same time I finished being my father's son."

"Uh, I'm not sure where you're going with that, but if your father passed away, I'm sorry."

"It was worse than death—I walked away from a legacy that meant nothing to me. My grandparents had struck it rich, and my parents, both heirs to wealth, were comfortable living that kind of lifestyle. I was raised by caregivers, sent to private schools, and taken on trips to see the world as a boy. I had everything money could buy."

I waited to respond until Philip was out of the cart and grabbing his club. "I don't know what to say."

"Nothing to say," Philip said as he pulled off the head cover. "I walked away; I told my dad and mom 'thanks but no thanks.' I had everything except loving, attentive parents. I had six nannies before I was thirteen. They were kind, but they weren't parents.

"I always felt that life was unfair when I was a kid, but it wasn't until I finished collage and gained some experience into how the real world worked that I figured it all out. Then I told my parents how I felt. To make a long, sordid tale short, they disinherited me."

I watched Philip take a few practice swings. It was as if he was slicing away some of the anger. But as he placed the wooden tee in the ground, he seemed to relax, and I heard the first pop of contact with the ball. The white dot lofted into the blue sky and dropped more than three quarters down the long fairway. It bounced twice, rolled a bit, and came to rest.

"You're up, Kevin," he said with a smile.

"All right," I said. "I see your mind is now in the game. Golf takes focus and my mind is still on your story."

Another excuse, I thought, as I addressed the ball.

After I made good contact with my ball, it doglegged right and landed a few inches from the rough.

"Golf is easier to straighten out than life." Philip consoled. "You'll be back on track with your next shot."

> **Golf is easier to straighten out than life.**

As we got back into the cart, it was obvious from all the chatter from the other cart that the ladies were enjoying each other's company. "Time to get up there, ladies." Philip shouted.

"You walked away from a legacy," I said still stunned by my misperception of the man. "That couldn't have been easy to do."

"Lots of money and lack of love from your parents messes with the mind. I had a tough time at school, even through college. People outside of my family never saw the real me; they only saw the net worth I represented. I thought people only liked me because I came from money."

While my wife teed up, Eva stood in front of Philip, "You're supposed to be watching us. You missed my drive! My ball ended up in the rough—your fault!"

The corners of Philip's mouth turned up as Eva laughed. Then instantaneously our heads turned to watch my wife.

"Stop looking at me!" she said. "Pressure!" Her swing mimicked Philip's, and her ball landed just behind his. She came over to the cart and took my hand. "Let me ride with Philip since we're in the lead."

Eva moved over in her cart so I could get in. Anticipating it would be a long day of golf, I took the opportunity to entertain myself with questions. "So, you guys met in college?" I said.

"Yes. It was more memorable for me than for him. I worked in the cafeteria in his dorm and watched him for a long time before he even knew I existed. I was nothing like him. I mean, look at us now—he's handsome, calm, and friendly. I tend to be an introvert until someone wakes up my voice. I'm either demure or on fire. That's why I enjoy working with your wife—she's easy to be friends with and she's a team player. She understands me and helps me pick the right fights. You must love being married to her. You even look alike," she said with a coy smile.

> ## I'm either demure or on fire.

After the first hole, Philip's score was par, and my wife trailed by a stroke. Eva missed two putts and I missed one more than she did, but the competition mattered less to me than the camaraderie.

I got back in the cart with Eva and on way to the next tee box asked, "What's it like to be married to a guy like Philip?

"In our first few years during college, I was intimidated by him," she said without hesitation. "His family was wealthy beyond imagination. On our second weekend together, he took me to meet his parents, and I actually got lost in their house. It was a horrible experience overall, but I had never seen such a place—they had a stable, a pool house, an archery range, their own forest land, and a stream that meandered through the property."

"He told me he walked away from that world. Did you have something to do with that?"

"No. Or, I don't think so. His sister set the stage for him to leave—she felt the lack of love from their parents even more intensely than Philip. By comparison, my family was supportive, even though the love had to be spread across six kids. We're such opposites. Philip had one sibling, and I have five."

"You are a handsome couple," I said. "You must complement each other in many ways."

"Thanks. But I'm not complementary to him when he works twelve-hour days. His work is his life. He's out to prove that he can be a self-made man. Even though I think he has proven it over and over, he gets up every day to do it again."

We arrived at the next hole, and this time Eva scored par. Then Philip announced, "Same people, same carts," and Eva and I went right back to where we left off in our conversation.

"What was your degree in?" I asked Eva.

"Education," she replied demurely. "I wanted to be a teacher, but I met Philip, got married, and worked at Williams-Sonoma for a year and a half until our son Ryan was born. Let me tell you, staying home with children is like being a CEO. Raising children is one thing; managing the business of a home is something else. Phillip works such long hours, and I decided to approach my work the same way."

Driving faster, she picked up the pace of the conversation, "When our kids get older, I'll get my certification to teach and start my career. Maybe we'll reverse the usual way couples do things—he can work in the house and I'll work outside. He can retire and babysit the grandchildren."

"I'm with you on that," I said, hoping for the day I could spoil a grandchild, "but right now, it's going to take work for us to catch up to our spouses because they are already on the green!"

On the next hole, Eva teed off. My wife and I stood to the side under a tree and she whispered, "So are you making friends with Eva, Kevin?"

"Yes, she's a nice person. I see why you enjoy working with her. Is it fun getting to know Philip?"

"Yes. I think after this we should hang out with them some evening. Philip has been telling me what it was like to grow up with absent parents. He told me his sister also walked away and never looked back. At least Philip still talks with them. He knows that, as they age, they'll need to have family who cares. He's a good son, but his sister is long gone from all of their lives."

"I hope Eva told you about how she and Philip are balancing work and family. They have an interesting take. Let me go back in the cart with Eva—you go with Philip."

Following my orders, I got into the cart. Philip was more eager to hear about what his wife said then the game or cart order. "So, what did Eva tell you about me?"

"She adores you, and from what I know so far, it's an amazing journey you two have been on. How about one of these evenings, you guys take a walk across that triple fairway over there and join us in our backyard for cocktails and appetizers?"

Philip took a drink from a water bottle. "That would be great. That's what I love about living here. You can take the boy out of his parents' mansion, but you can't take the country club out of the boy," he laughed.

> **You can take the boy out of his parents' mansion, but you can't take the country club out of the boy.**

"We always dreamed we could afford to live here on our own dime," Philip continued. "We paid extra money every month on the mortgage of our first home, even though we'd stretched to buy it in the first place. When we started our family, we found a great deal on the house in here, but it needed a lot of work. Eva stayed home with the kids and spent the next several years fixing it up to meet the value of other homes on the block."

"While you continued to work long hours, right?"

"When the mortgage handlers plunged us into crisis, my company suffered a major downturn," Philip said softly. "I had to cut costs—and employees. Our property and financial investments went down, and we needed to stop putting money into the pension and college funds. If I could have worked twenty-four hours a day, I would have!"

Philip stopped and, with his Maui Jim's staring at my Ray-Ban glasses, said, "I've worked so hard at my job, and still I have been a better father to my children than my old man was to me. Let me tell you, doing that takes a lot, but having Eva as my wife is like having the power of the sun at my side."

> **Having Eva as my wife is like having the power of the sun at my side.**

Arriving at the next short par 3, Philip turned to me and said, "Ask me something else before the next shot—something about beer or food. Talking about that old life is not conducive to setting up my next hole-in-one!"

"That's my strategy," I laughed.

With that, Philip pulled a nine iron out of his bag, traded it for an eight iron, and walked over to the tee. He took about a minute and a half to set up, and then he drove the ball long and straight. I immediately stopped regretting the can of unpleasant worms I'd gotten him to open and start thinking about how I could beat his drive.

My shot was decently long but not as straight as his. As I got back in the cart, I thought about Philip's story and about other people's preconceived notions about their country club neighborhoods. The reality was, most residents there had overcome adversity in order to move into their dream homes.

Having walked away from family money that would have made his financial life simpler, Philip was self-made like most of our neighbors. I could tell that he and Eva were not fools who borrowed to the hilt for material satisfaction. They'd shown me how logic, balanced emotion, and orientation toward action could accomplish any goal.

My mind then drifted to what my wife and Eva might be discussing—details about the event they'd planned, no doubt. And although we'd only exchanged pleasantries, I found Eva to be more casual in demeanor than her husband. Given her volunteerism, she showed equal strength in her sense of responsibility.

By the ninth hole, we had caught up to a foursome waiting in front of us, and we declined to play through. We had parked our carts pleasantly in the shade of an ironwood that was showing its age. Because of what Philip said about working hard to be a good father, I mentioned reading an article I had written about how the American Dream that our generation envisioned in grade school wasn't feasible for most mid-to-late Baby Boomers, Gen Xers, or Millennials.

Eva leaned over to be in earshot of our conversation and said, "I'm afraid for our children. I don't know what to teach them, although I know education of values comes from family, society is so strained these days."

She looked at Philip and continued, "My husband had a complicated inner world during his teenage years. He was a follower. His social image of 'having it all' was a thin facade that masked his sensitive, caring soul. His sister helped him confront his parents, walk away from them, and make his own life. Me? I started with nothing, but I trusted that working, saving, and being responsible would bring gains and a good life, even if I had to wait for them."

> I trusted that working, saving, and being responsible would bring gains and a good life, even if I had to wait for them.

As Eva spoke, I noticed how Philip seemed delighted with his wife. He said, "I watched Eva picking up trays and wiping down tables, in that cafeteria. She would undo her bandanna to bunch her hair, standing in front of the tables with that long thin body like she was walking on stage. It was hot. Then one day when my so-called friends left me to go to class, I stayed behind, and that's when I first saw Eva smile."

Hearing those words, Eva's face became as bright as the aurora borealis. "I was nothing like him," Eva said, trying to contain her joy. "I was kitchen help, and he was a big man on campus. My dirty apron and hair scarf were the exact opposite of his starched oxford, pressed khakis, leather belt, and loafers. But when I smiled at him that day, he whispered, 'Thank you.'"

Philip remembered well. "I had felt all alone at that big table, but her smile turned that into a feeling of being the center of someone's world. From that point on, time moved quickly. We spent every free minute together as we watched people around us move in slow motion. Eva knew my heart. She saw the real me; she saw past my reputation."

Time had stopped for the foursome, too, and I looked lovingly at my wife.

Unaware of the larger impact of what he was saying, Philip continued, "After the cafeteria job, she worked at a hair salon, and she even insisted on paying for some of our dates. After graduation, I promised Eva I'd work endlessly for the two of us and our family, if things went that far. And that's the story, right there."

"Time to pick up the pace of this play, you guys."

"We know that's not the end of the story!" my wife commented. "Eva, come sit with me and tell me all about how he proposed."

"Yeah, Philip, she's right. What did you do after you graduated?" I added.

Philip was quick to reply. "I don't know how many times people told me, 'You'll never make it without your family's connections,' but that made me want to work even harder. I drove a delivery truck just to make ends meet with all the enthusiasm I had—same way I'm about to drive this ball. Excuse me for a minute—I have a date with a tee!"

With another powerful swing, Philip led us back into play. As the ladies teed up, Philip told me back in the cart that the delivery truck job had him at the wheel for only a short time, because the owner, soon recognized his work ethic and moved him into management.

Eva and Philip had spent years to become financially independent. Three and a half years after they graduated, they were married in front of a small group of friends at the courthouse in Tacoma, Washington. Philip told me their lives after the wedding were filled with challenges, mostly because they tried to save what little they didn't spend. Saving was critical to their success. However, their peers were borrowing to spend what they didn't have.

> **Saving was critical to our success.**

"We were both working very hard," Philip pointed out as he stepped on the pedal, jolting the electric cart. "After we married, instead of living in an extravagant place, we downsized, lived on my salary, and banked hers."

"A logical approach," I said. "Very few people embrace that attitude. Instead, they subscribe to the popular image of marriage and acquire a bigger home, better cars, and all the extras. That lifestyle results in enslavement, because it limits options down the road and people don't grow financially."

We paused for a moment to look at the score cards. Philip remained quiet, so I continued.

"Many people feel empty even when they appear to have it all because that kind of immediate gratification often ends in disappointment, an inadequate nest egg for retirement, and sometimes even divorce."

Philip looked up thoughtfully. "Lots of people we know are divorced. It's filled with drama, trauma, and the costs are astronomical—in money and in emotion."

"Approaching a marriage or any partnership in the way you did gave you the power of two," I added. "You generated a one-plus-one-equals-three result, and it should translate exponentially in future years."

"Well put, Kevin," Philip said. "You're right. We stuck to this simple rule: stay committed to a task that's beneficial in the long term and make personal adjustments as needed to align with that long-term goal."

"Many marriages could have benefitted by your rule, Philip," I concluded.

> **We stuck to this simple rule: stay committed to a task that's beneficial in the long term.**

Philip's posture straightened, but he bowed his head slightly. "We took a class at church and learned the best thing we could do was not take on debt except for the kind that grew equity, like a house. It was a hard mental transition to make, especially when we had solicitations every week for new credit cards. But we told ourselves we would buy a house and pay off the mortgage as quickly as we could while we were still young. It's something Eva and I will teach our children to do, too."

As we rounded the back nine, my mind was on the state of the country and how lenders dragged out home mortgages for thirty years to guaranteed predictable income streams, keeping customers shackled.

Adding fuel to Philip's story, I said. "The start is often the most exhilarating part of a dream. You and Eva used that power to take the high road. You made marriage a powerful asset to overshadow challenges."

As our golf cart hit a bump, Philip grabbed the wheel tighter and said, "We reminded each other that frugality was an advantage in itself. It brought us closer together, which in turn made our lives richer and our struggles smaller. Over time, that mindset has worked like a charm. We moved up professionally, traded up to a nicer home, and honed our relationship."

"Funny," I said. "I often see that people's broken emotional bonds fuel their attachment to physical things...because they believe those things will make them whole."

We hit another bump and, grabbing the sunshade, I pondered how Philip and Eva moved like waves through life's obstacles as they focused on the beauty of their lives and not useless objects.

"Hey, daydreamer," Philip broke into my thoughts. "We're here, you're up!"

Tired of playing golf, I slowly walked back to the group after I teed off as they were finishing a conversation.

"We don't look for happiness in material things," I could hear Eva say. "When I lose track of us, I slow down and make sure I put Philip before the rest. Doing that helps us feel safe and secure." With that she glanced at her husband.

Philip smiled and said, "Having kids was a huge awakening, but again, it boiled down to hard work and a team effort every day.

Eva stays home and takes care of the foundation of our lives. If I didn't have that, I wouldn't know what to do."

My wife motioned Eva to get back into the cart as she said, "You had that good hard work ethic from an early age."

"Without a doubt!" she replied. "It takes restraint and a great deal of practice, but practice is what cements learning, and we practiced every day."

> ## Practice is what cements learning, and we practiced every day.

She continued, "It's like being on a diet that forbids dessert. The temptation is always there to eat just one sweet treat. If you weaken once, the next time becomes a little easier, and the next time even easier until your diet doesn't exist. Those who can resist temptation find satisfaction in a reward that goes far deeper and lasts much longer than a donut."

Philip walked over as he clipped the end of his cigar. Without looking up, he lit it with a slow burn and said, "We also practiced by setting a goal of buying only what we believed was essential. At the least, we had to have money in the bank to pay for a purchase. We did without a lot of extra stuff that often ends up gathering dust anyway."

"Not like a good cigar," I laughed, grabbing the lighter to fire up a fat one.

On the fourteenth hole, my wife was up first. As she set up her shot, the rest of us reviewed our score cards. We had slowed down a tad on our pace, which made me think that, in all aspects of life, there's a natural tendency to fall back. There's no fighting gravity—at least on planet Earth. So why not put extra effort into whatever you do to get an edge—be it in love, school, finances, or the last five holes of golf? It was time for me to put some extra effort into my game.

Psychologists say the world is an extension of the brain's perceptions. When used to its best advantage, it gives people control of their destiny by providing an understanding of how they think and, thus, how to act. As I took several practice swings, I considered what thought patterns work for Philip and Eva. When setting personal and financial goals, they assigned both long-term and short-term benchmarks to track where they were and adjust their expectations.

> They assigned both long-term and short-term benchmarks to track their performance and adjust their expectations.

Now I needed to find some benchmarks for my one small goal—a good performance on this par 3 hole!

I teed up. Everyone was quiet, so I took the cue and shushed the voice in my head. I approached the ball, zeroing in on it, and then I felt my muscles tense as the club rose into the air above my head. The swing gathered momentum, and the clubhead hit the ball, indicated by that most perfect sound and punctuated by the whoosh of the follow-through.

We watched the ball sail toward the hole.

"Niiiiiiice!" Philip said. "You're going to walk on that green with an edge."

"Work hard to play hard," my wife said.

"Hmm, those are two things I love," I smiled back. "Let's go have our short game." As we moved closer to the green, Philip grabbed his water, and I again was lost in thought.

The kind of work ethic Philip talked about is essential to making the country great. It's one that has made millions rich.

Unfortunately, after more than two centuries, work ethic had given way to expecting benefits without work.

When we got to the edge of the putting green, my ball happened to be closest, so I jumped in and played it out for birdie, making it my best hole of the day so far.

"Well done. You're working it now," Philip said. "Working hard always gets returns."

As our wives finished the hole, Philip, still eager to share the secrets to his self-made fortune, shouted, "Credit!" Then behind a big puff of smoke, he said. "Now, there's a topic for you. About a year ago, I was denied a line of credit despite my good qualifications. I know it was due to the national trend of irresponsibility in which people traded more credit for less work, but I felt slighted."

Philip's cheeks slightly reddened. "But it's okay for the *government* to overindulge. Politicians acted like they could fix the recession, yet they were the ones who started it in the first place. I mean *come on!*"

Eva, who'd finished the hole in five strokes, chimed in, "When your dog digs a hole on someone's lawn, you don't look the other way and say, 'Some other dog did it.' But that's what they do in Washington. Government and the ever-expanding public sector have forgotten who they work for."

I invited Eva to sit in my cart and sent Philip to my wife's. As we drove to the next tee box, I said, "Government depends on hardworking taxpayers for its existence, and that makes me angry. But you and Philip knew how to turn anger into change. It's a revolution that puts a personal agenda of family economics first so that pork-barrel politicians and corporate giants don't feed themselves on regular folks."

> You and Philip knew how to turn anger into change.

"Darn right!" she said. "We're saying no to exploitation and refuse to contribute to campaigns unless politicians prove their qualifications."

"Yes, to me a politician's ability needs to be equal to those of professional executives I've had the honor to work with," I said.

My words seemed to have struck a chord with her, because over the next several holes, she elaborated on her beliefs about taking responsibility, not blaming others, and the weakness of excuses. She finished by saying, "People often avoid the truth about themselves."

I was enamored! But my truth right now was the two scratch-golfers in the cart in front of us. They were on fire.

After watching Gretchen and Philip hit great shots off seventeen, Eva grabbed her club and said, "You and your wife are a good match, Kevin."

"Not in golf," I replied humbly, "but in life."

"She was the one who demanded full transparency on the school board," Eva added. "And has me working my tail off on this fundraiser. Now I'm trying to catch her handicap on the course!"

We both laughed with a sense of exhaustion.

"I think I'm done for the day," Eva finally admitted.

"Me, too. Time for refreshments."

We decided the outside patio would be the perfect place to reminisce on the day so after hurrying through eighteen, we proceeded directly to the clubhouse.

There we all sat together basking in warm conversation and fun laughter about our day on the links. Eventually, the sun became a fleeting colorful spectacle at the end of the distant fairway. Seeing its brilliance, Philip leaned over, kissed his wife, and gave her a lingering hug. In that moment, the sun dropped below the horizon, and I heard her faintly whisper, "Another American Dream come true…"

> **The sun dropped below the horizon, and I heard her faintly whisper, "Another American Dream come true…"**

We said our good-byes and agreed to spend more social time together. As Gretchen and I drove home, I took her hand and said, "During our young lives, the world as it had been then taught us many lessons. It was a struggle adopting spiritual momentum as a personality trait, but we always got through the bad times. So, tell me again that poem about rain you love, the one by Longfellow?"

"Oh, yeah," Gretchen responded. "Something like, 'Into every life some rain must fall.' But he didn't specify what quantity of rain to expect."

We squeezed each other's hand.

"The amount is different for everyone," I said. "What is consistent is that situations have no emotions, so how we react to them can put a positive spin on any challenge."

My wife looked thoughtful as I continued, "No one talks about this, but friendships are investments, too. I think Philip and Eva will become good friends of ours after today."

"Oh, I agree," she said. "Constant digital bombardment often leaves us cut off emotionally from human connection, and it can crush the God-given magic that beckons people not to be afraid to love. Staying surrounded by others who share the essence of what brands humankind is what keeps all of us grounded."

> **Staying surrounded by others who share the essence of what brands humankind is what keeps all of us grounded.**

Once we were the garage, my wife took off her seatbelt and turned to me, saying, "Eva is one of my favorite people. Not because of what she has accomplished but because of her openness and warmth." "The perception that Eva and Philip have it easy is an illusion. They work hard, struggle, and face challenges just like everyone. Times usually get harder than you expect, which is why having a long-term plan is essential."

"You're brilliant darling," I lovingly acknowledged as I concluded that individuals can make their dreams happen by discovering what works for them in their long game.

You too can use Secret Success Standards from Philip and Eva's life story like the ones below as stepping-stones to your own accomplishments:

- Work hard and save money to be successful. Be frugal and don't take on debt (except the kind that grows equity such as a house).
- Your dream can come true if you work at cementing the discipline required to make hard choices.
- Every day, commit to tasks and adjust them as needed to align with your deeper ongoing goals.

CHAPTER 11

Unleashing Success

*Most men who long to be rich know inwardly that they will
never achieve their ambition.*
—James Hilton

D o not stop now! You too can achieve the successes that
others in this book have done. Stepping-stones have
brought you to this final chapter, and you understand—
maybe for the first time—how ordinary folks do extraordinary
things to attain riches. You've seen firsthand how they've done
it without dishonesty or malice, yet they've achieved wealth in
inspiring ways. You've witnessed circumstances that invoked
spiritual productivity for people to achieve their highest goals.

This book shows that by choosing to live authentically and
connecting your personality to the vastness of your spirit, you can
achieve the abundance you want.

Whatever insights and motivations you were seeking when
you started exploring these life stories are now yours to exercise.
You can have your desires simply by creating a unique formula
commensurate with the infinite possibilities of your spirituality

and personality. Take the bold move to close wealth disparities by living on your own terms and refusing to be part of the agendas of self-serving individuals, megacompanies, or deceitful politicians. Step into your own driver of financial independence and become financially free.

Rely on Knowledge that's Exclusively Yours

By reading the stories of these heroes, you've seen a groundbreaking perspective on wealth-building based on the less-traveled paths of the Quiet Rich. You can now use that perspective to unlock your own success standards, connect them to your goals, and implement sound practices to create both temporal and emotional wealth.

Ignore experts touting one-size-fits-all, get-rich-or-your-money-back guarantees. Those techniques typically are theoretical and reflect personal bias. Such unproven strategies are being sold for the monetary gain of the originator, but they're like a shoe that won't fit your foot.

Instead, rely on the knowledge that's exclusively yours. It will fit like a glove as you learn from those who have already attained wealth on their own terms. Let your intuition lead you on an exclusive journey customized for you alone.

> **Let your intuition lead you on an exclusive journey customized for you alone.**

You'll define Secret Success Standards for your own consciousness and will organically guide you into action. That is the only effective method for achieving abundance.

Right now, take inventory of all the things that make you the person you are. Then, let go of anything that does not honor or serve you and begin your revolution.

Your Transformation Starts Here

Many self-made millionaires were reared in families or cultures that believed money was not an end that justified the means. That kind of thinking could have led to a stigma that becoming rich crossed wholesome family values and pitted currency against courtesy. Such ensuing conflict might have robbed them of the transformation that inspired their first million.

They, however, redirected the noisy chatter about those who found success at the expense of others. Instead, they pursued wealth in a way that was morally acceptable to them. As their stories revealed, they achieved an outcome that suited them well.

Before you take another step, realize you hold your own spiritual supremacy. It is what predisposes you to becoming rich. Using the ideas in this book, you can define a path based on your own values as your "I can" message takes you to a new level of success and wealth.

The Four Cornerstones of Prosperity

In whatever you do, living the four cornerstones of the Quiet Rich will bring you prosperity on whichever path you choose. Use these four cornerstones as the foundation that holds your financial dream structure in place.

Throughout this book, you recognized the values underlying every chapter. They also appeared in the hundreds of case studies compiled in the research after which the analytical method used to write this book was modeled.

The four cornerstones are:

1. An intuitive belief that you are here on earth for a greater purpose.
2. A knowingness that you are bound by moral responsibility to others.
3. A realization that dreams can be manifested, but fantasies don't come true.

4. An unwavering work ethic that links your daily journey to high achievement.

Upon these four cornerstones our heroes built their personal success standards that guided them into becoming individual powerhouses. Learn these four cornerstones. When you employ them often, they will serve you always.

The Financial Dream Architecture

To make your goals more quickly attainable, your next step is to build your achievement architecture. Use the primary themes from each chapter to frame your strategy by sequentially connecting the precepts illustrated and listed for each chapter.

Learn them one at a time, then make them your principles to guide your actions. In this way, you'll start building an architectural structure for your success.

Healthy Self-discovery

In **Chapter 1: Roads to Riches**, you learned that *knowing yourself* on the continuing journey to making your dreams come true must start with openness and truth about *who you are* behind all the walls of protections you might build.

Thomas knew only what he saw and never strayed far from his center of thought in Boston. However, once he traveled out on the open road, his mind gained the openness of the highways. Like Thomas, having honesty in admitting *who you are* is the benchmark for growth. That truth opens you to benefit from experiences you would otherwise dig in your feet to resist.

Once he opened his mind, Thomas realized he needed to find solutions that worked best for him by discovering how he could move seamlessly through life instead of being paralyzed by fear. Some people will not look objectively at themselves or their situation. They stay miserable because they decide the misery they *know* is better than what they have yet to discover.

However, facing yourself, accepting who you are, and letting go of what doesn't honor you ultimately makes you a better person. It's like driving down a dark road at night. You only see what's in front of the headlights, yet an entire world awaits to be illuminated on the periphery.

Along the path to achieving your dreams will be portions of the road you can't see. That's okay. What matters is that you stay on your path, remain open, and love yourself and the healthy journey of self-discovery.

Doing your best can only come when you know what is best for you—and when you realize you must first know who you really are inside.

Power of Uniqueness

In **Chapter 2: Broke Not Broken**, you realized there is a *supremacy in accepting who you truly are*—meaning not what shows up in public but the real you. Hiding things or keeping one's idiosyncrasies private is not abnormal, while some unique characteristics may seem hard to accept. However, never be ashamed of who you are; you are that way to serve a greater purpose. Remember, there is no one quite like you!

Shaun's mantra was accepting "amazing me," which moved him to focus on self-acceptance and overcome personal resentment. When he celebrated to celebrate, he was able to engineer methods that worked for his uniqueness rather than wasting precious energy on regretting what he was not.

Similarly, you can gain the self-confidence you need by facing your fears and taking action. Everyone carries baggage from the past, be it from parents, lovers, or environments. No one gets to adulthood unscathed, but don't spend the rest of your life trying to fix things. Move on!

Refuse to engage in personal conflict. Rather, find full acceptance in *who you are* and *who you can become*. Resolve to move forward by breaking free of the past and then run toward the future.

Follow your inner voice and shut down the critics in the back of your brain by becoming a neutral evaluator—as Shaun did. To do this, make sure you follow your passion and not the expectations of others. That means focusing on the process and knowing it takes time and patience.

Purposeful Possibilities

In **Chapter 3: Pockets of Wealth**, it was clear to Judy that *happiness and promise abound* in life. She saw the good around her, then she applied skills of motherhood and homemaking to identify products she trusted. From there, she amassed wealth in the stock market.

Similarly, don't miss the advantages around you or fall into drudgery during daily routines. All you need to do is look for the bountifulness surrounding you—as Judy did. Start this change by recognizing your journey is not about distance but about moments of consciousness and internal awareness. For example, no one knows exactly when a disease is cured, but it can happen in a split second. Miracles are found within, making the possibilities *endless*.

Always be present in your life and never take it for granted; this is the greatest gift of all. Move through your day with immediate purpose knowing *the now* that holds the greatest potential. It is the most powerful indicator of future gain.

Learn to tap into the investment pool of tangible or intangible possibilities that exist around you. Use this technique to amass any kind of capital—financial, personal, spiritual, intellectual, or social—that will make your dreams come true.

Mostly, be aware of your environment, use what you know, focus on what you can control, and manage your expectations.

Doing Away with Fear
In **Chapter 4: Wings of a Plan**, Peter faced all odds and made adjustments to do away with any fear he felt. Over time, he not only solved problems but found excitement in addressing new challenges. Just as a deer freezes in a car's headlights because it's out of its normal environment, things we don't expect happen in life.

Fear is the greatest detractor from potential, and it leads directly to confusion and lack of action. Roadblocks are inevitable, but when they occur, many people stop in their tracks afraid of what lies ahead. Peter, though, anticipated obstructions and managed his fear by being ready for them. He stayed nimble at all times and created contingency plans to combat any surprises he faced.

People become lazy because it's easier to be afraid than accept ownership of all the consequences. In that sense, fear can be an opioid that is easily adopted. It can even open the gates to being slothful. That's why it's best to turn fear into action!

Peter knew that he consistently needed to make hard decisions in accordance to his environment to best provide for his family. His sense of being accountable displaced any fear and stimulated changes that would benefit him. Peter also took charge of his own life without contemplating others' criticisms.

Making decisions based on someone else's point of view is never good and often results in an inferior outcome. Making decisions based on fear is worse. Instead, transform your bad breaks into opportunities, given that how you handle fear and adversity ends up defining you—molding you a shining suit of armor to take on any challenge.

Fortitude, Dignity, and Perspective

In **Chapter 5: For Richer, for Poorer**, Jack recognized the world was bigger than what he had known as a boy in a small town. By transcending limiting beliefs, he used the experiences of those around him to release his full potential.

Letting go of the narrow corridor thinking of his youth, he climbed to a higher point in his mind to see a global perspective and newfound purpose. Jack became aware that the safety of his small-town community was nothing like the big city where he encountered people who would take advantage of him. Some would even hurt him for their own benefit. With that perspective, mixed with the integrity of his childhood, he was able to become equipped for creating new ways to challenge his competitors. Rather than being attached to specific outcomes, he committed to his own strengths and value set.

Old patterns of thinking *seem* safe, but they are actually feeble excuses that keep people from trying something better. Jack was not accustomed to having unsavory people on the farm, but he quickly learned to deal with them directly in order to succeed. He knew doing something because "that's the way it was always done" is a recipe for failure. Instead, he used his strength to oppose his competition but still maintain his core value set.

In this story, Jack used fortitude to change how he interpreted the world, and he adjusted accordingly. As a result, he could adequately address the toxicities of his rivals in his own way— before they invaded the stability of his business.

Jack left behind the small town of denial for a bigger approach to challenges but stayed committed to the ideals he valued. Like Jack, you must rise above the fray by *being true to your word*, both with others and yourself. When you learn to be aware of threats around you, then you can see them as new opportunities and take decisive action.

Focused on Fulfillment

In **Chapter 6: Inner Compass,** Drew focused on defining what worked best for him, then *gauged his actions to keep him on that bearing.* He overcame personal loathing of his own poverty by immersing himself into the mainstream American culture. That way, he made the most of his experiences, *good and bad,* to heighten his own development.

In fact, the social deprivation that came with starting his life in abject poverty allowed Drew's devotion to creating financial freedom to naturally fall into place. That meant accepting where he came from and striving for who he needed to become.

Drew used this new culture to gain a broader perspective for new ideas and advantages. Concurrently, he didn't let others distract him from his determination and ability to gauge what worked best. He developed a practice of *going home* with his decisions while letting others go home with theirs.

Some people don't advance because they lose sight of their commitments. Drew kept focused by internally tracking his own fulfillment and measuring his progress—with the goal of becoming a better human being. His brain acknowledged his past, but his soul guided him to future fulfillment. He addressed the day-to-day problems by teaching himself to embrace uncertainty. At the same time, he played the long game and used events associated with poverty to keep pursuing a better place in life.

Opportunities in Diversity

Chapter 7: Myself in Others emphasized the benefits of *accepting the never-ending canvas of people and possibilities.* Each one of us has unique skills and perspectives. Choosing which of the myriad possibilities that would benefit our cause to financial freedom becomes the challenge.

As shown by the cousins who provided exponential value to each other, a good team reaps never-ending benefits from embracing differences. Exchanging ideas through verbal communication is a powerful way to solve problems and come up with new ideas. Conversation is the medium of conscious propositional thought with feeling, thinking, and talking being intimately linked.

Without concrete examples, abstract logic occurs through language. Thus, an endless pool of people is waiting for you to access their thoughts; all you need to do is talk to them. From there, you can manage your relationships through appreciation and applying clear directives.

Matthew and his cousin differed from each other but worked through their differences without judging each other. Judgment comes in two flavors—to make yourself feel better at someone else's expanse or to see what potential lies beneath your differences.

When it came to finding solutions, the cousins used objective reasoning to weigh their options. They created opportunity by discriminately asking, "What if?" and they learned from their mistakes by applying key lessons to future ventures. In effect, their dissimilarities became a 1+1=3 equation. Similarly, always be on the lookout for your strength to come from the power of opportunities in variances.

Truth and Self-validation

In **Chapter 8: Dancing to a Heartbeat**, Jane pulled herself up by her bootstraps by validating *who she was* and *where she needed to go*.

Self-betterment won't happen unless you accurately assess the truth about the world and how it responds to *you* so you can set goals. If you lie to yourself about who you are or about a situation because it hurts your feelings, you will never grow. Not making a decision is the biggest you'll ever make. The only thing that stops you from making mistakes over and over is building memory muscle from resistance.

If you don't seek truth to avoid the pain, you lose the exercise for gain and can never self-validate.

Jane knew she could choose how to effectively engage in competition based on who she was. But she first needed a true read on both. She was able to change her approach or avoid doing something that didn't work because she saw things as they were and knew who she was by assessment.

When you take ownership of all that happened, you can adjust your approach in a way that works. Jane categorized what was truly important in herself and was able to self-validate with those qualities to keep her in the game. In doing so, even when people tried to compromise her ability she could compete with her personal brand of integrity.

There will always be disruptions, but tenacity is a learned trait. Put on blinders to the negativity of others and let your passion lead to a way that's indigenous to a beautiful you. When you discover something isn't working, be honest and correct the course. Changing a course of action is not failure. Instead, realize the distinction between "knowing" and "believing," understanding that believing carries a percentage of doubt.

Vision of the Future

In **Chapter 9: Of Humankind**, Brandon *embraced wealth and success* by maintaining a long-term focus on the future. He was no athlete, but he kept his eye on the ball or, specifically for him, the prize.

Some people see only part of an equation and keep missing the answers because they push closer and closer into their tiny world, forgetting that like the universe, possibilities are limitless. Brandon stepped back to see the whole landscape to comprehend all the moving parts and how they might apply to his bigger long-term plan. He used practical knowledge nontraditionally to free himself from the pain of his circumstance, knowing it would benefit him—in much the same way he did as a child.

During his professional climb, Brandon knew in his heart what he could become, even when surrounded by associates whose status gave them the advantage over him. He systematically used a scientific method of observing, questioning, and concluding to train his mind. He never accepted people were better than him or were entitled by their history. This helped him overcome any childhood disadvantages, and he gained a strength that eventually translated into future achievement.

Like Brandon, never lose sight of your goal. Just as a paint brush adds color and definition to a canvas, you can use your unique talents to develop the image you want.

Embrace wealth and success, visualizing how it will look on you some day when they are yours. You will realize results if you can see them ahead of you.

No one can see what you see the way you do, so make that your advantage and use your insight to build a long-term dream. Always state and envision your desired result as you commit to your desired endpoint in a finite time by setting deadlines. That way, you will re-code your mental game with positive self-talk as you program your subconscious mind through visualization.

Connecting Core Drivers

In **Chapter 10: Fire and Water**, our heroes show that internal motivation comes from *accepting challenges and taking small steps* to meet, adjust to, and overcome adversity.

On their financial climb, Philip and Eva used sacrifice like a game, and it resulted in sound monetary decisions. Frugality became a benefit and brought them unexpected success. Not having money was less problematic when they viewed it as the potential to gain wealth.

To do without takes discipline, but once you accept the potential benefits, it becomes easier—even an incentive. Philip and Eva were different personalities, but together they found a balance in each other's weakness and strength that gave them the power to achieve greater goals. Much like athletes, they blended their core strengths to adjust and improve their performance. Similarly, you have core attributes that are uniquely yours that make certain things easier than others.

It takes discipline to straighten your wings in a blowing gale, but that is what allows you to soar higher. Let things that work against you become an advantage by connecting all your best abilities as needed. Learn to neutrally adjust and let go.

The golf clubs used for long distance are called drivers. Other clubs are designed for short, more accurate maneuvering of the ball. Just as a golfer chooses the right club for a particular shot, choose your "clubs" carefully. Become familiar with your core drivers, use them properly, and let them hurl your success higher.

Take all the shots you want that come naturally to you. If a "bad" event happens in your life, do not judge the world as a hurtful or horrible place and withdraw from it. Ships sink not because there's too much water around them but because there are little holes that have gone unaddressed. Fix your mistakes by using what comes naturally to you and making your journey easier.

You can learn to live large if you see your limitations as the place where creativity begins, and motivation takes over. Let adversity lift you into financial overdrive!

Take a Quantum Leap Toward Your Results

You have already witnessed the limitlessness in which the Quiet Rich made spiritual connections to their personality and translated them into actions. You felt similarities with them because of the spiritual bond all people share. Now it's time to personalize their Secret Success Standards or create your own.

To do this, go back to those chapters that had commonality with your personality and highlight what resonated with you. *These are tactical takeaways.* Write them down along with what you expect to receive from using them. Adapt your criteria to the actions as you put fine finishes on your financial dream structure. This lasting combination will always guide you.

> ### This lasting combination will always guide you.

Every morning, read your notes aloud while commanding your subconscious "I will attain success my way." When you look at the words, breathe deeply and free your mind to assimilate the action-oriented messages that stimulate your verve.

Revisit your list as you go about your day and keep it with you to read in private moments. At the end of the day, re-read it and remain still. Allow the items on your list to connect with the vastness of your spirit and arouse natural changes in your brain as you sleep.

> ### Allow the items on your list to connect with the vastness of your spirit and arouse natural changes in your brain as you sleep.

Did you know your brain has an ability to form new neural connections to change your life? It does! In time, you'll see your practices work. After forty days, you'll begin to master new ways to wealth. Then one day, in a quiet moment, you'll realize you have created your own version of financial freedom among the Quiet Rich.

Actions to Achieve Greatness

Practice your new actions every day. Science has shown that daily action is cumulative. Meditation, even two minutes a day, helps reduce anxiety and increase creative energy. This can stimulate an internal wherewithal to avoid distress and allow change to come from within.

> ## This can stimulate an internal wherewithal to avoid distress and allow change to come from within.

Participate in positive efforts toward your goals every day, even if it's only surveying the stories that you love the most.

Some days, you will feel full of ability, and other days you'll feel weary. Regardless of how you feel, though, pull from within and visualize your desires and results. External doctrine starts with acting, feeling, and authentically living—from within. That is the simplest way to your greatness.

Here are key actions to take every day:
- Carry Primary Objectives
- Actualize Secret Success Standards
- Move with Crystallized Intent
- Grow, Change, Transform

Finally, keep the Secret Success Standards you most identify with, what you expect to receive, and the personal criteria for action with you. This is your action list.

> ## This is your action list.

A to-do list rarely goes unaddressed when it includes tasks that take you closer to your dreams. When you doubt yourself, put your hand in your pocket or purse and touch it to physically attach to it. Over the course of a day, continue to write down creative feelings that come to mind. This will also prevent you from projecting anger and frustration while helping you direct thoughts toward responsible actions. This is the best use of your own capital process flow. You are your own spiritual guide, so trust yourself and do what impresses you!

> You are your own spiritual guide, so trust yourself and do what impresses you!

Secret Success Standards Will Actualize Your Dreams

Develop your own Secret Success Standards as you grow. Words of encouragement alone won't build your confidence to achieve. Instead, create a clear picture in your mind of what you will be doing, with whom you will be doing it, and in what ideal situation. This will self-actualize your dreams.

And always watch for signs so you can observe how far you've progressed.

As you visualize your actions as intentions, you'll find realization of your dreams through new connections of spirit and personality. When you do this, the energy you emit will attract the effectiveness you need to accomplish your mission as you apply your unique talents.

The only thing that can truly build confidence and achievement is personal action. You'll find that when you align your Secret Success Standards with your values and dreams, your confidence will soar.

> When you align your Secret Success Standards with your values and dreams, your confidence will soar.

A sole survivor of an airplane crash was looking for a doctor to remove medical hardware fused in her back after years of recovery. The operation carried risk of paralysis, so she avoided having it done. One day while walking through an office park, she passed a doctor's office and saw photos of airplanes on the walls. She walked in knowing she was in the right place. She listened to her intuition and worked with a doctor who knew what was needed in her situation.

Watch for signs throughout your day-to-day activities. Change will be like driving from a crowded city to the country. Terrain along the route will change. Traffic, steel, and concrete will dissipate as they're replaced by greenery and wildlife.

Your direction to attainment will also have recognizable changes that mark milestones in achieving your goals. Reaching them should not drain you or cost you power. Done in your own way, you will lose track of time and focus only on the journey.

> **Done in your own way, you will lose track of time and focus only on the journey.**

Constantly Grow, Change, Evolve

Measure your progress every week. Create a worksheet to help you recognize that you are growing toward your goals. If a task isn't working find another way. If that doesn't work, move to something else but keep going until your energy is flowing toward your goal. Your spiritual and personality will always show you where to go.

> **Your spiritual and personality will always show you where to go.**

Once you've achieved a behavioral change that benefits you, don't fall back into old patterns or relationships that drain your energy or prevent you from soaring. Move forward with the change. Never stop progressing or setting new goals.

Remember, security comes not from having financial wealth or expensive items, but from the totality of resolving ongoing issues to your benefit. Evolving in yourself in such a manner naturally induces action that empowers a new you.

Go Forth and Prosper

Now, it's time to prosper on your journey to greatness and financial independence. Be aware of purposeful occurrences and soon you will be among the Quiet Rich. Emulate the secrets in this book to unleash your own potential, build your internal dream, and climb the ladder to whatever success you desire. You are on a personal quest for your American Dream.

May your journey be exceedingly rewarding!

AUTHOR'S NOTES

I realized it was time to stop obsessing about "millionaires on steroids" and celebrate those making up the majority. The ones, as my dad reminded me, who embody the values this country was founded on—hard work, honesty, and integrity.
—**Kevin J. Palmer**

On a Thanksgiving trip back East to my parents' home, I listened to my father's version of how our country's social values have embarrassingly declined. "People today," he said, "can't seem to create wealth without the help of corrupt schemes."

I sensed sadness in his voice. The lessons he and mom taught us were based on treating others the way we wished to be treated. If we did, we'd inherit the earth and all that is in it. Of course, my parents' advice was overridden with realities about expecting nothing for free and working for our dreams. Reaching them any way other than through the esteemed moral values with which we were raised would not be acceptable.

During dinner, my father went on about how America's biggest corporations were paying CEOs incomprehensible salaries and bonuses as big as lottery winnings. At the time, I had been advising NYSE member firms on improving their business models and knew the slogans printed on the coffee cups weren't the way people conducted business.

But to keep my conscience clear, I reminded Dad that even though we hear about super-rich individuals gaining wealth on the backs of those barely managing to stay afloat, more people were quietly prospering even in the cruelest of times. And they were doing it in honest ways. In fact, most ordinary men and woman I uncovered during my research at a behavioral-finance firm had based their paths on old-fashioned ethical standards.

Dad reticently admitted that he and mom may not have done our family justice when it came to making millions by omitting the eye-for-an-eye, tooth-for-a-tooth lessons of business, perhaps inadvertently denying us a fair chance against unscrupulous members of society.

"I don't begrudge Chas down the block for having a Cadillac. "I'm happy with my Chevy. Every American deserves the right to build his dream without interference or oppression."

Mom interrupted reassuringly. "We're fine. We have the most important things life can provide—a close-knit loving family, the integrity of hard work, and decency in our purpose."

Reflecting back on that conversation, I realized Dad's uncharacteristically cynical attitude compelled me to take a meticulous look at the people who did financially surpass others.

Data on Achieving the American Dream

As the research unfolded, it astounded me. The cases of success *without compromising values* were far more numerous than I'd ever imagined, and the people themselves were more interesting than movie heroes. It soon became clear that I could help improve the human condition by sharing my data so those who put in the effort, could achieve their own version of the American Dream.

The community in which I was reared was like thousands across this great country. It had an interesting mix of white-collar and blue-collar families, and everyone seemed to have a big enough piece of the American Dream pie to feel content. If someone was in need, people came together to help. Our neighborhood might have been considered an affluent bedroom community of New York City, but no one seemed to feel entitled. There was never talk about who was welcome—or not welcome—to live there. People fit by being a responsible part of the community's character.

My town of hardworking, connected people produced famous and not-so-famous offspring who remember it as a great place to grow up. People there, like citizens of similar towns, based success on simple honesty and the hard work that enabled America to become the world's greatest nation.

Crossing the Economic Rubicon

Today much has changed. When I visit places like it, I see communities that have become about "where I live" and "how much I make," regardless of how their neighbors are surviving.

Unfortunately, the media focuses too much attention on billionaire headline-grabbers and their grinding greed of one-upmanship—even though their numbers actually total only in the hundreds. Media does not highlight the millions of families who quietly work toward the kind of dream-come-true prosperity that makes America great. Missing until now were the amazing stories like those from my roots about the cornerstones of economic prosperity. The people who use their own notes, octaves, and melodies to make rich music in uniquely quiet—yet enormously prosperous—ways.

Core of Human Greatness

I believe my dad was right. By living lessons of simple, honest success, average folks can become financially victorious—because in the consciousness of humankind, spiritual wisdom is at the core of true human greatness. The proof lies in the amazing stories of contemporary success in the pages of this book, were hundreds of like-minded people explored their own divine uniqueness and created a righteous path to riches.

ACKNOWLEDGMENTS

Leadership comes from the ability to apply accumulated experience under the incidence of battle.
—SMA Institute

Deepest gratitude and thanks to:

My dear wife Gretchen, daughter Rachel, granddaughter Sophia, my parents, siblings, and extended family and friends.

All those at Strategic Mgmt. Advisors, The SMA Institute, and SMA Institute Ltd. who crystallized opportunities of America's birthright.

The many who encouraged, inspired, or worked on this book, not limited to:

America's Forefathers
Analysts at the SMA companies
Dr. Carl Gustav Jung
David J. Palmer, PhD
Dawn Palmer Trahey, M.A.Ed
Diane Palmer Cornel, RN MSN
Gretchen L. Palmer, PhGD
Isabel Briggs Myers
John Monteleone
Katharine Cook PhD
Mary McCaulley, PhD

Pamela Chambers M.Ed.,NCC
Dr. Ransom Rogers
Dr. Robert Sideli M.D.
Robert Shiller, PhD
Barbara McNichol
Yvette Romero
Tiffany Gibson
SMAI Research Group
Unnamed many who came forth with research,
points of view and opinions

SIGNATURE PAGE

A s you close this book, think of being rich as "having a great value or an abundant supply of something," then choose what that means to you.

ABOUT THE AUTHOR

Devoted to peace through prosperity, Kevin J. Palmer is a financial industry veteran challenging economic injustices through empowerment. In the stock market, only the most astute analysts can predict early and accurately that a ripple is about to become a tsunami and he made such calls on numerous occasions.

His proficiencies are deeply rooted in driving performance for Wall Street giants Merrill Lynch and Paine Webber. After leaving the broker-dealer industry, he served as Managing Director of Strategic Management Advisors, where he collaborated with other executives to build better securities firms during a financial paradigm shift.

In 2008, to drill deeper into his *98-percentile hypothesis*, he spun off the SMA Institute. There, using scientific method, combining graduate studies in finance, with psychology and social work degrees, he dramatically altered socioeconomic forecasting and investment policy modeling.

Measuring scope and scale of emotional intelligence in cognitive decision-making, he uncovered how people create wealth and make financial choices. The resulting behavioral and monetary insights opened barriers to attainment for ordinary people everywhere.

His public advocacy against economic abuse resulted in methods to advance morally achievable wealth. That collection of work continues to disrupt the debate about wealth-stratification and economic inequality.

In his free time, this champion of financial justice participates in wildlife rescue and environmental stewardship, and as recipient of the Governor's Archaeology Award, he is fascinated by uncovering the lives of individuals who lived thousands of years ago.

CPSIA information can be obtained
at www.ICGtesting.com
Printed in the USA
LVHW030154261120
672694LV00022B/533